From the Heart of a Leader
PRINCIPLES, MEDITATIONS, AND SERMONS FOR LIFE APPLICATION

By Presiding Elders of the African Methodist Church (AMEC)

E. Anne Henning Byfield, General Editor

From the Heart of a Leader:
Principles, Meditations, and Sermons for Life Application

Copyright © 2020 by AMEC Publishing House
Published by the AMEC Publishing House (Sunday School Union)
Nashville, Tennessee

www.amecpublishing.com
All rights reserved. No part of this publication may be reproduced, stored in a retrieval system, or transmitted in any form, except for brief quotations in reviews, without the written permission from the author or the publisher.

Printed in the United States of America

First Printing 2020
ISBN: 978-0-929386-28-7

DEDICATIONS

To the first Presiding Elders of the AME Church,

Thank you for your sacrifices, commitment, and legacy!
Because of you, we are!

The Rev. Dorothy Millicent Morris, Guyana, 16th Episcopal Church
The Rev. Helen C. Patrick, Suriname, 16th Episcopal Church
The Rev. Cornelia Wright, 3rd Episcopal Church
and
Rev. Dr. Eyvonne Whitman, Presiding Elder

The principles were compiled in this book with you in mind as one who would be a contributor. You are the quintessential gift of leadership as a pastor, presiding elder, and a friend: You have demonstrated the elegance of a profound woman, an amazing leader, and a generous spirit. We thank God for your overwhelming anointing from the Holy Spirit, which was shared with so many. Your transition to our divine Creator did not allow you to participate directly in this project, but we decided that your legacy is already included in diverse ways.
We miss you, Dr. Eyvonne Whitman.

Rev. Margaret Fadehan, Presiding Elder

We are grateful that you were able to participate in this project before your sudden transition to our Creator. Your leadership as a pastor, presiding elder, and a connectional officer is noteworthy and significant. Women and men around the global church listened and learned from you. The Church saw a leader who was African and woman. I also saw a compassionate, committed leader who shared with me serving as daughters of presiding elders. Your contribution to this book serves as another part of your rich legacy.
You are loved and appreciated, Rev. Margaret Fadehan.

To All Presiding Elders serving in the Connectional AME Church

CONTENTS
PRINCIPLES, MEDITATIONS, AND SERMONS FOR LIFE APPLICATION

By Presiding Elders of the African Methodist Church (AMEC)

Dedications..2

Foreward..5
The Right Reverend Dr. Carolyn Tyler Guidry

Preface..7
The Right Reverend E. Anne Henning Byfield

Introduction: 9
The Reverend Marilyn A. Miller Gill...12

Chapter 1: 13
God Made You a Leader (Know You Have the Right and a Vision to Lead)
The Reverend Dr. Betty Holley: Principle 14
The Reverend Valarie Walker: Meditation/Sermon....................19

Chapter 2: 23
Transformative Leadership Principles that Work

The Reverend Dr. Letitia Watford: Principle 24
The Reverend Dr. Fran T. Cary: Meditation/Sermon..................30

Chapter 3: 35
Excellence in What You Do

The Reverend Dr. Janet Sturdivant: Meditation/Sermon 36

Chapter 4: 47
Living Beyond· Ministry or Leadership in Your Personal Life (Having a Life Outside the Life of the Church)

The Reverend Margaret Fadehan: Meditation/Sermon 48

Chapter 5: **52**
Leadership While Living in a Drought

The Reverend Dr. Elaine P. Gordon: Principle 53

Chapter 6: **58**
Principles I Wish I Knew Early in Ministry

The Reverend Dr. Rosalyn Coleman: Principle 59

The Reverend Jacqueline Smith: Meditation/Sermon 63

Chapter 7: **66**
Living a Ministry of Servant Leadership

The Reverend Darlene Smith: Principle 67

The Reverend Carlene Sobers: Meditation/Sermon 72

Chapter 8: **76**
Balancing Compassionate Leadership

The Reverend Dr. Brenda Beckford Payne: Principle 77

Chapter 9: **82**
Learning from Failures

The Reverend Linda Faye Thomas-Martin: Principle 83

Chapter 10: **85**
Finishing Strong

The Reverend Rosetta Swinton: Principle 86

Contributing Writers **91**

Bibliography **96**

Endnotes **99**

FOREWORD

At the beginning of my ministry, spanning forty-five years to-date (as of May 3, 2018), I was determined to be the best I could be wherever my assignment took me. I envisioned that path as only in the role of Pastor. As a life-long member of the African Methodist Episcopal Church, I was indeed familiar with the position of Presiding Elder (PE). However, in 1973, I did not know any women who had ever served in that capacity. By 1994, when Bishop Vinton R. Anderson appointed me as the first female Presiding Elder in the Fifth Episcopal District, I was one of at least five female Presiding Elders in the AME Church, including one in South Africa.

I am honored to be asked by my Sister Bishop, the Right Reverend E. Anne Henning Byfield, who joined me as the second woman who served as Pastor and Presiding Elder before being elected Bishop, to be a part of this endeavor. There were also two men elected from the position of Presiding Elder before us, the Right Reverend Vernon R. Byrd, Sr. and The Right Reverend Zedekiah L. Grady.

Most people in the Church, if asked concerning the duties of the Presiding Elder, would probably reply very quickly, "to collect Conference Claims." However, *The Book of Doctrine and Discipline* sets forth a more detailed set of duties for this critical office, intended to provide oversight of congregations during the Conference year. This oversight also includes training for Pastors, Officers and Members via District Conferences, and Sunday School Conventions, as well as Data collection at Quarterly Conferences.

There are also times when the Presiding Elder must also serve as Pastor to assign the pastor or congregation. The *Discipline* no longer requires that the Presiding Elder should preach in each congregation, but the PE, like every preacher, must always be "ready to preach." So, the following principles and meditations will come from years of sermon preparation and study, as well as the experiences of years of Leadership.

Thanks to Bishop Henning Byfield, for providing a platform in this book so that those men and women who serve as Presiding Elder will be able to "speak" to generations to come. It is my prayer that this book of Leadership Principles, Sermons, and Meditations will encourage all who aspire for excellence in ministry.

The Right Reverend Carolyn Tyler Guidry
122 Elected and Consecrated Bishop of the African Methodist Episcopal Church, Retired

PREFACE

The idea of the *From the Heart of a Leader* had its genesis when I served the Church as a Presiding Elder. I was surprised at the lack of understanding of the Church for what a Presiding Elder does, and at a depth of leadership contained in the office of a Presiding Elder. Moreover, there was a flawed conception of leadership principles in general. My years as a Presiding Elder revealed that one of the by-products of this misconception is reducing the office of a Presiding Elder to simply a mid-manager, a person who is a paper shuffler, and money handler.

To facilitate growth at the Presiding Eider's district and to strengthen leadership at the local church, "Preparing Leaders for Leadership" was born. This conversational training empowered members to understand the depth of their leadership giftings to stimulate growth and to respect the critical need for a Presiding Elder.

The role of Presiding Elders is a complex and strategic position in the life of our Zion. The Presiding Elder is first a shepherd who identifies and enables other leaders to be leaders in the local church, which helps the Chief Shepherd to have oversight of ministers, laypeople, and the church in the district.

Working with Presiding Elders demonstrated that they had a heart for leadership, and much of what is done by them is to empower leaders. Leadership is not gendered-specific, and neither is the office of the Presiding Elder. Women were selected for this book to provide principles of leadership for leaders. They were also chosen because, as a Presiding Elder, I understood even in this glass ceiling appointment, women were often hard-working, productive, and successful leaders without some of the benefits and recognition of male Presiding Elders. Like many in the church or corporate settings, glass ceiling appointments for women are not always in strong districts with large churches and great financial perks. After years of successful pastoring, the promotion often pays less than the church they pastored but with greater challenges. Nevertheless, they are effective and efficient and committed to the ministry.

Who, then, is adept at offering principles from the heart of a leader to leaders than these exceptional Presiding Elders who, along with their male counterparts, provide a profitable undertaking for the Church? As you read, you will realize that this is not a women's leadership book, rather a book for leaders written by leaders who are women.

Every principle in the book is applicable and relevant to leaders and in life. This book is both theoretical and practical from leaders who serve both as leaders in their profession and person. Learn from these leaders to become better leaders.

We give credit to the many who have helped make this book a reality. Thanks to Rev. Lucinda Burgess and Presiding Elder Betty Holley for listening and shaping the original idea, and thanks to Reverend Marilyn Gill for editing, proofreading, and serving as the administrator. A special thank-you is extended to every contributor who amid quarterly conferences, annual conferences, planning meetings, sickness, family emergencies, and other responsibilities found energy and time to complete their assignment. But in the final analysis, I shoulder the responsibility for all its weaknesses and give God praise for a competent team.

This book is dedicated to all of you who are called by God to be leaders and serve the people of God.

The Right Reverend E. Anne Henning Byfield

INTRODUCTION

A Collection of Stained-glass Leadership Principles, Sermonic Reflections, and Meditations

Many leaders dare not accept positions without establishing a clear vision of their expectations, along with a definition of their role as a leader. In doing so, many may investigate to discover the origin of the word "leader." According to *Holostictoolkit.com,* the term *lead* assumed a new definition from its Indo-European source and the "prehistoric West and North Germani *claithjan,*"during the medieval period. Today, a less complicated definition from various etymological sources simply equates to this: that a leader, while having the capacity to affect others, not only can see one's vision but is also able to follow one's vision.

Nevertheless, as Christians, one is summoned to emulate an even higher standard of leadership. Jesus desires fruitful Christians to follow him the way he followed God (John 15:1-11 NRSV). Hence, as a Christian leader, one must not only follow Jesus but also must lead others, as one is being led by Jesus. Further, leadership is combined with God-given talents (natural spiritual gifts), and God-given responsibility (accountability), which the authors of *From the Heart of a Leader* developed during their leadership roles. These talents and responsibilities have enabled them to develop and lead others. Subsequently, their contribution to this book illustrates that these writers are keenly aware of God's purpose in their lives and the template they are to emulate. They are skilled at influencing others in their unique ways of leading, while God continuously prepares them for leadership. I have observed that when appropriate leadership principles are practiced and shared "decently and in order" (1 Corinthians 14:40), it follows the expectations of Jesus. Such leadership principles recommended practices, and sermonic reflections can be discovered in *From the Heart of Leader*.

The idea to share such invaluable leadership principles from Presiding Elders of the African Methodist Episcopal Church is timely for such a time as this. One will be able to glean from *From the Heart of a Leader,* the significance of authentic leadership styles while observing and contrasting today's rebranding of leadership styles by the 45th leader of the United States of America. God's pattern of leadership is uniquely different from the worldview pattern of leadership. God mandates that leaders are to be accountable, accessible, and available to God. Leaders must depend on God rather than on social media, the press, and other secular sources.

Of significance, the leadership styles that God has revealed to us from our biblical ancestors remain fundamental to Christian leaders. These leaders include Moses, Huldah, Debra, Daniel, Esther, Nehemiah, Ruth, Mary, Phoebe, daughters of Philip, and Junia, the Apostle. Along with these biblical leaders, God uses Presiding Elders of the African Methodist Episcopal Church, who exhibit strong leadership to those they lead. Many of them have proven that they are courageous like Moses; scholars like Hulda; prophetesses like Deborah, true to their God-like Daniel; risk-takers like Esther; ordinary but determined like Nehemiah; and available like Mary of Magdalene; servants of the Church like Phoebe, Phillip's daughters, and Junia, the apostle.

Of further significance, these presiding elders are leaders who lead from the inside out. Their inward alignment is the organized master key for their outward leading and guiding of others. Leading from the inside out allows one to share one's most intimate experiences, i.e., fears, challenges, doubts, and other emotions and incidents. This outward sharing of the inward alignment is one of many fundamental principles that decision-makers consider when one is to be elevated to a position of organized leadership.

Organizing is also a luxury skill for any leader. One who possesses organizational skills is among a unique class of leaders. Whether it involves organizing one's life, one's thoughts, one's ministries, one's family, or other focus areas, the organization reveals a sense of structure to the final product. Organizing requires that one sometimes must go the extra mile to reach the first mile. Organizing mandates that one visualizes the end from the beginning for the image of a perfect outcome (Isaiah 48:9, 10). Hence, how one organizes one's personal life, as well as how one shapes one's values for public view, will determine how others portray one and value one's work as a leader.

From the Heart of a Leader will awaken you and equip you to lead or continue to lead. This resource is packed with stained-glass leadership principles, sermonic reflections, and meditations from the strengths of women writers who continue to make a difference in leadership. Key leadership principles are revealed in each chapter: God Made You a Leader, Leadership Principles that Work, Living While in a Drought, Principles I Wish I Knew Early in Ministry, Living a Ministry of Servant Leadership, Balancing Compassionate Leadership, and Learning from Failures. Other sermons, meditations, and reflections stand on their strengths: "Excellence in What You Do," and "Living Beyond Ministry or Leadership in Your Personal Life." The content in these pages provides an invaluable asset to mature ministry, lay, and auxiliary leaders, students, and counselors. Overall, *From the Heart of a Leader* is intended to bless the reader. It is my prayer that this unique collection blesses the men and women who take the time to read these pages that these anointed leaders have shared.

So many women leaders have blessed us. In every religious sector, there are those who not only exhibited leadership but made changes in the lives of many. Rev. Jarena Lee was the first woman authorized to preach by Richard Allen, the founder of the African Methodist Episcopal Church. She established many churches and schools and traveled to New England. Her courage brought forth a great crowd of witnesses of women in African Methodism and beyond.

All honor is also due to the late Reverend Prathia Hall Wynn, who pressed her way to become one of the first women ordained by the American Baptist Churches, USA. She was a prominent and incredible Civil Rights leader who labored with the Student Non-Violent Coordinating Committee (SNCC). The Right Reverend E. Anne Henning Byfield has afforded other women, ministers, and laypeople opportunities to soar and lead like never before.

I am abundantly grateful for the opportunity to contribute to, *"From the Heart of a Leader."*

Reverend Marilyn A. Miller Gill, Managing Editor
Associate, St. John's Missionary Baptist Church
Executive Director, Indiana Christian Leadership Conference
Indianapolis, Indiana

CHAPTER 1

God Made You a Leader
(Know You Have the Right and a Vision to Lead)

"Lead...you are already a leader."

annehenningbyfield

"To whom much is given much is required."

Jesus

GOD MADE YOU A LEADER

Principle

Betty Holley

There are several domains for the principles of leadership. The domains that will be discussed include the following: a personal relationship with God, personal character, relationship skills, organizational skills, and motivation. These domains represent leadership principles of a truly transformative leader in Christ; irrespective of gender, the transformative leader will be discussed throughout this chapter. For our purposes, transformative leaders seek to inspire, empower, and propel others to excel by using their gifts, skills, and talents. Transformative leaders ask the overarching question: why would anyone want to be led by me? To answer this question, a true leader of Christ must inventory their competencies by asking several questions of themselves and be genuine in the responses they hear deep within. Questions along this line might include the following: can I communicate with care? Do I exhibit a genuine passion for throwing light on my commitment? Am I an encourager of others' participation? Do I know how to praise others, which promotes my ability to build others? Am I able to get others excited about their work? Do I possess any teaching skills? Am I vision-oriented? Do I know how to create positive working environments for persons placed in my care? Am I a true team player? How's my time management skills? What skills do I possess to enhance another's self-worth? What safeguards do I have in my DNA to avoid micromanaging? Am I always prepared? Do I know how to network? Have I embraced transparency? Do I make myself accessible? Do I exhibit self-confidence? Am I a life-long learner? These are not all the questions that need to be answered by leaders of themselves, but it is a good start. How one responds to questions of these types determines the answer to the over-arching question: Why would anyone want to be led by me?

One must possess an impeccable personal character, which is another principle of a transformative leader. A personal character must consist of three competencies: resilience, integrity, and emotional maturity. These three competencies must always be maintained to be able to exemplify true personal character. Having a personal relationship with God is a paramount principle for transformational leadership. To have a personal relationship with God hinges on possessing an unwavering faith that will be tested by an unfailing God. A faith that cannot be tested by God; God cannot use it! In the vicissitudes of life, there will be challenges to confront every day in the lives of God' s people. What will be the response of the leader to critical challenges when people need to be uplifted to gain the courage to run another mile of the way? When the horrific incidents occurred at the killing of nine AMEs at Mother Emanuel on March 17, 2015, the recent killing of eleven Jews at Squirrel Hill on October 27, 2018, transformative faith leaders had to step forward to demonstrate genuine faith through their words and deeds to console the hurting hearts of family and friends near and far. These faith leaders exhibited discernment and obedience to God in using their faithfulness to give people hope and a reason to hold on to God's unchanging hand.

Resilience enables one to handle disappointment and rejection while maintaining effectiveness. We are all susceptible to rejection. Just because we are who we are, as we work in our various roles of leadership, does not give rise to being given the gift of immunity from types of rejection—sexism, classism, racism, just to name a few. Resilience is the ability to bounce back against all the odds. Effectiveness is one of the principal markers of resilience. Therefore, our effectiveness must always be intact regardless of the circumstance to demonstrate resilience.

Integrity is the second competency to help hold our personal character above reproach. Integrity enables a leader to adhere to godly values in personal and professional life. A leader without godly values is not a leader at all. Without integrity, a leader, whether transformative or not, has no trustworthiness. Without trust, everything the leader does comes under higher scrutiny. Integrity is the glue that holds the leader to the expected standard for an impeccable character.

Emotional maturity, the third competency, demonstrates the leader's ability to understand and manage their emotional state while helping others tunnel through their valley situations. When situations go awry, there needs to be an adult in the room. The transformative leader must be able to hold everything together when everything around is crumbling. These three—resilience, integrity, and emotional maturity—must be firmly in place to always present the leader with unquestionable character.

Leadership is all about relationship skills building, another key principle. Authentic leadership cannot exist without relationships. Therefore, relationship building skills are of the utmost importance when operating in a leadership role. A transformative leader must be able to develop appropriate skills to work effectively with others in the Church and community. To work collaboratively with others is the only effective way to bring about lasting change. Appropriate relationship-building affords transformative leaders to keep Christ at the forefront when dealing with adversarial situations and foster reconciliation.

Organizational skills, yet another key leadership principle, aid in decision-making, delegating, and empowering, along with planning and organizing. Excellent decision-making skills are needed to identify and analyze given information to draw an appropriate conclusion for a given situation. A transformative leader must be able to transfer responsibility to others, recognizing their gifts, skills, and talents to deal with situations, thereby empowering them to serve. Transformative leaders seek opportunities to empower others to assume the responsibility of leadership. Excellent planning skills help to establish the leader's ability to organize procedures to complete their work efficiently and effectively. Without excellent organizational skills, the work of a transformative leader becomes mute.

The critical domain for this list of principles of leadership is motivation. Motivation speaks to the heart of a transformative leader. There are several elements of motivation that make transformational leadership possible. Loving God is one of the vital factors that enable motivation. Without love for a God that makes all things possible, motivation is impossible to achieve. Motivation is intrinsic and comes from within. If the leader does not love God, then there is nothing within. Loving God will allow the leader to possess a servant's heart, an element of motivation. Only through a servant's heart can a leader have a desire for service. Desire is a product of motivation. Desire pushes one to explore a greater need for service to offer humankind. Loving the Church is another element of motivation. The Church, within and physically, is a leader's God-given gift to work out God's "calling." Working out the call serves as a motivator to love The Church more with each passing moment. Love for The Church enables a transformative leader to take on challenges for church transformation. Loving The Church allows a leader always to be engaged in missional thinking that drives the work of God's congregations all over the world. The most compelling element of motivation is empowerment. Motivation pushes transformative leaders to go and empower others to become laborers in the vineyard. We are called to "go" and make disciples, according to Matthew 28:18-20, the Great Commission. To go and empower others, motivation must give us the push we need to hit the highways and byways, compelling others to join in God's great work.

Serving in a leadership role as a PresidingElder, program director, professor, mother, grandmother, has given me experiences in leading to allow me to speak from the heart throughout this chapter. Leading others in any venue is a sacred task, in my view. God allowed me to touch persons' lives through various roles of leadership that have enabled me to be a better leader. Transformational leadership is reciprocal. Reciprocal is an agreement or obligation bearing on or binding each of the two parties equally. Drawing on my mathematical background, which is where I tend to reach to give a more explicit explanation in helping to make my meaning clearer for me; reciprocal as a mathematical expression or function is so related to one another that their product is one; the quantity obtained by dividing the number one by a given quantity. Transformational leadership allows for reciprocation, mutual relationships. A reciprocal relationship is developed through the principles of transformational leadership. Everyone gains. Everyone becomes better able to do what they have been called to do. Change can become evident in a transformative reciprocal relationship, the change needed to make this world a better place for everyone, and God can get all the glory!

In summary, we have come so far; yet we must continue moving forward to impact change, locally and globally, from the White House to the church house. Transformative leaders are needed that possess a moral compass and ethical values guided by the God of the disinherited, the God of disenfranchised, and the God of the people on the margin. We cannot afford a recrudescence of violence from the '60s, voting privileges for persons of color, and the rights of women.

GOD MADE YOU A LEADER

Meditation/Sermon

Valarie J. Walker

Then God said, "Let us make humankind in our image, according to our likeness; and let them have dominion over the fish of the sea, and over the birds of the air, and over the cattle, and over all the wild animals of the earth, and over every creeping thing that creeps upon the earth." So, God created humankind in his image, in the image of God, God created them; male and female he created them. God blessed them, and God said to them, "Be fruitful and multiply, and fill the earth and subdue it, and have dominion over the fish of the sea and over the birds of the air and over every living thing that moves upon the earth" (Genesis 1:26-28, NRSV).

From the foundation of this earth, almighty, awesome, sovereign God, creator and sustainer of this great universe made you a leader. God created us in God's image and likeness and blessed us with the Spirit of righteousness and love, "The Spirit of wisdom and understanding, the Spirit of counsel and might, the Spirit of knowledge and the fear of the Lord" (Isaiah 11:2).

As humankind populated the earth, God called and used male and female to lead by taking God's authority and commanded us to be fruitful and multiply. God's image and likeness is the very essence of who you are, spirit, soul, and body, a powerful trichotomy vessel of God, endowed with God's purpose, power, and passion, to lead God's people to green pastures and the still waters. God created everything and everybody on purpose, with purpose.

Life has a greater meaning, a greater fulfillment, and a greater joy when we allow God to lead us in finding purpose. "God saved us and called us with a holy calling, not according to our works but according to

God's own purpose and grace. This grace was given to us in Christ Jesus before the ages began" (2 Timothy 1:9).

God's leaders are called, chosen, and consecrated as witnesses to the purpose, power, and passion of Almighty, an awesome, sovereign God. God's leader understands his or her position in the Kingdom of God because God's leader is called by God to be out front for God, to serve and guide with the Spirit of excellence, to be totally effective and efficient. As God's leader, you cannot settle for mediocrity. You excel in leading and managing God's program, God's property, God's provisions, and God's people.

God raises up leaders for God's purpose, with power and passion for fulfilling God's command from the very beginning of time, "Be fruitful and multiply, fill the earth, subdue it and have dominion." God made you a leader to be used by God to allow his Spirit to govern, rule, influence, and control the earth. From the foundation of the earth, humankind was equipped and empowered with every skill, ability, capacity, strength, gift, talent, and anointing you need, to lead and serve humanity. Thus, letting your light shine before others, so they may see your good works and give glory to your Father in heaven. Our light, our spirits filled with the Holy Spirit shines forth in a dark, dismal, depressing, and devastating society to bring hope, healing, liberation, peace, justice, and righteousness.

The human mind cannot grasp the vastness of the command given by God at the time of creation. In us is the very essence of God's being, God's Spirit, God's power, God's authority, God's righteousness, and God's love to lead God's people to higher heights, deeper depths, and greater works. Jesus proclaimed to God's leaders, called Disciples, "Very truly, I tell you, the one who believes in me will also do the works that I do and will do greater works than these because I am going to the Father" (John 14:12).

God's leader will see themselves as Disciples of Jesus Christ, with a greater sense of servanthood, manifesting in them to do the more excellent works. The time is now for the greater works; God Made You a Leader to bear fruit, more fruit, and much fruit. We are connected to the True Vine.

God's leaders have already been cleansed by the Word of God. You who abide in Jesus and God in you will bear much fruit because apart from God, you can do nothing. God made you to bear fruit, to spread the gospel, to deny yourself: to take up your cross and follow Jesus. Our mission is clear. Jesus said, "The Spirit of the Lord is upon me because he has anointed me to bring good news to the poor. He has sent me to proclaim release to the captives and recovery of sight to the blind, to let the oppressed go free" (Luke 4:18).

God made you a leader to further the work of the kingdom. God is calling you to stand firm, to exercise, *exousia,* our delegated authority and liberty, and to exercise the full power of attorney in all of God's interest. God's complete authority in you is to lead and act in God's stead as if God were here doing the work. God is calling leaders like Joshua to be strong and courageous, to have good success, and lead God's people to the promised land. God is calling leaders like Esther, who was all in, "If I perish, I perish," leaders willing to surrender all to save God's people.

God made you a leader, like Richard Allen, the leader of the African Methodist Episcopal Church, who stated, "I am somebody. If you would just let me finish this prayer, I will not bother you anymore, and I'll worship under my own vine and fig tree where I can worship in dignity." Our vine and fig tree are all around us. God has blessed us to accomplish, build, create, envision, and acquire, more than all we could ask for or imagine, according to the power that works in us.

God made you a leader, like Reverend Jarena Lee, the first woman authorized to preach by Richard Allen, our founder of the African Methodist Episcopal Church. She was a great leader to be admired, who was called and challenged, yet lived a courageous journey. She stated that she wishes to unite these people. People are looking for leaders to lead and to draw them closer to God, to answer their call to preach the gospel.

Lead with integrity, intimacy, intensity, and intentionally. This chaotic and challenging world needs you. There is gun violence, anti-immigration, voter suppression, voting rights for felons, lack of economic opportunity and employment, safety, security, well-being, human trafficking, climate change, government accountability, transparency corruption, inequality, discrimination, and the Coronavirus. God made you a leader, to take your corner of the mat of this crippled and paralyzed society and "be fruitful, multiply, fill the earth, subdue it, and have dominion."

God made you a leader to advance and enlarge the borders of the Kingdom of God by spreading God's liberating gospel, the "good news" of love, mercy, grace, forgiveness, salvation, sanctification, justification, and glorification. As God's leader, accept the call and the challenge to rise up, take a stand, run this race until we see God face to face. Therefore, God's leaders are to be steadfast, unmovable, always abounding in the work of the Lord, for as much as you know, your labor is not in vain. **"God Made You a Leader."** God made you a leader, the Greater is within you!

CHAPTER 2

Transformative Leadership Principles that Work

"It is what it is, but it does not have to stay that way.

Effect change... leader."

annehenningbyfield

THE PERSPECTIVE OF A PRESIDING ELDER IN THE AFRICAN METHODIST EPISCOPAL CHURCH

Principle

Letitia Watford

The call to transformation, "But, be transformed..."
(Romans 12:2)

The over-arching goal of the Church is to advance the reigndom of God—to be that *body* where God rules and where God calls its members according to God's purpose. In his seminal and itself transformative work, *Experiencing God,* Henry Blackaby teaches, "God is always at work."

Those subject to the reigndom of God will necessarily seek to discover where God is at work, and then join God in that work. God *knows* the attainment of this lofty goal requires the transformation of those comprising the Church as their minds are renewed (Rom. 12:2). God calls out leaders to intentionally guide others through this transformation, resulting in their embrace of and contribution to the advance of God's reigndom.

Transformative leadership *causes* transformation (WikiDiff). According to experts, the transformative leadership model borrows its best practices from across the spectrum of varied, other models; to include transformational, charismatic, level 5, principle-centered, servant, and covenantal leadership models. Of these other five models, that which is *transformational* inspires followers to raise the bar for self, seeking to benefit the individual while enhancing organizational outcomes. That which is *charismatic* inspires unprecedented results through a well-articulated and compelling vision, which transcends self-interest for the good of the whole. That which is *level 5* calls for a certain humility along with a resolution within the leader, to reach previously unattainable outcomes. That which is *principle-centered* adds value, does not harm, treats others as valued ends, rather than a means to an end. That which is *servant leadership* demonstrates an authentic concern for the welfare of others. That which is *covenantal* brings a teacher, model, exemplar, truth-based perspective to the belief that only through increased understanding can people benefit themselves.

Raising the Bar – "(God's) ways are higher than (ours)"

(Isaiah 55:8-9)

God's ways are higher than our ways. As individuals comprising the body, we all are still on the journey to somewhere higher. The transformative leader takes the matter quite seriously and, beginning with self, seeks to go higher in the things of God. All the while, the leader is encouraging those comprising the body to go and do likewise. In this regard, the transformative leader is also a *transformational* leader and, by its definition, leading the way to transformation. The process begins with the acknowledgment that there is a "higher place" both practically and spiritually. Jesus is our exemplar. Where Jesus is, there is God. God reigns where God is. God is a God of excellence. Therefore, the transformative leader strives for excellence (not perfection) in herself, continually encouraging each member of the body to pursue the same in themselves, to the glory of God, and the advance of God's reigndom.

The Vision Thing – "Write the vision; make it plain."

(Habakkuk 2:2)

Where are we going? How do we get there? Why do we want to go there, anyway? In pursuit of the reigndom of God, none of these are genuinely relevant questions. The far more relevant questions are these. Where is God leading? How would God have us to proceed? Who would not want to go there? Wherever God is presently leading, it is to a new place, and it will manifest in a God-sized outcome. A God-sized outcome requires that those who follow be inspired to come aboard, perhaps to go where they have never been, probably by means they have never before utilized. The subjugation of personal agenda and personal druthers for the sake of the whole may be required. The *charisma* of the transformative leader is not so much a personality style or trait, as she can offer a clear, compelling vision of the where to, the how-to, and the why of the next steps—all of which (ideally) align with God's will, God's direction, and God's way. Having realigned themselves to flow with the articulated vision and within the parameters set for its accomplishment, what transforms both the leader and follower is the seeing-what-God-can-do that results in the believing-what-God-can-do.

No 'I' in Team – "In humility value others above yourselves." (Philippians 2:3)

The transformative leader calls self and others to excellence, calls self and others to subjugate their desires and ambition to those of the common good, to achieve previously unattainable outcomes. Now, while the transformative leader exudes a "get 'er done" spirit and his dedication to "see the mission through" is unquestioned, he fully appreciates there are no lone rangers in God's economy. Traversing from a God-sized vision to reality will be a very arduous ascent, but teamwork makes the dream work. Ideally, each team member carries their loads, making themselves available to bear another's burdens. Ideally, they row together, simultaneously, and in the same direction. The transformative leader shares in both the resolve and the humility of a *"level 5"* leader. A leader among leaders, he values his team members *and* their inputs, acknowledging *both* at every opportunity, as God speaks to him *and* to those that God brings to God's work.

Walk the Talk – "And this is love, that we walk after (God's) commandments" (2 John 1:6)

In leadership theory, a *principle-centered* leader has this "highly ethical obligation to honor implicit duties owed to others" (Covey). There is this moral duty to add value, not harm, and to contribute to the welfare of individuals and society in the future (Caldwell et al.). The transformative leader who is devoted to advancing the reigndom of God strives not only to uphold but to impart principles and values consistent with God's precepts and Jesus' example.

In the context of the Church, the transformative leader is a disciple who makes disciples. Conventional wisdom has it more disciple-making is caught than taught. Therefore, the transformative leader, who is also a *principle-centered* leader, will strive to adhere to the same values and principles espoused before others. That leader will walk after God's commands, as she leads others in the same way. That leader leads in accomplishing God's ends, God's ways, all the while appreciating it is not really about the event, the program, or the building, but it is always about the advance of God's reign in the lives of both the leader and those she leads.

Come to Serve – "Even (Jesus) did not come to be served, but to serve…" Mark 10:45

Genuine *servant leadership* intersects with transformative leadership in its commitment to team members. The welfare of those who follow supersedes the welfare of the leader. While never suggesting that the transformative leader is another's doormat, the transformative leader nonetheless retains an elevated opinion of and appreciation for those he leads. The focus is on the needs, desires, interests, and welfare of others, above personal self-interest (Ludema and Cox). However, when in the pursuit of God's reigndom, the call of the transformative leader to servanthood equates with the call to help those s/he leads better delineate needs vs. desires, interests vs. callings, and self-interest vs. God's interest. The call to servanthood is a "down and dirty" one: Witness Jesus' washing the disciples' feet. Servanthood is a call to relationship one-on-one, as well as in small groups, which can be tedious, even messy. However, when the benefits are manifest, transformation results. In the best of situations, servant leadership is paid forward. The transformative leader will find that those in whose lives he invests will, in turn, invest in the lives of others.

Teach! "So, a church leader must be able to teach." (1 Timothy 3:2, NLT)

Transformation results from a change of mind, attitude, and action. However, one does not know what one does not know. Therefore, of necessity, a transformative leader is a teacher. In the Church, the role of the transformative leader coincides with that of the *covenantal* leader, in that both such leaders will teach and model a truth-based perspective, lending itself to the renewing of minds, the changing of hearts, and the resulting congruent actions and reactions. The best of teachers is intentional, systematic, and remediate as needed.

The best teachers are also the best learners. As a leader among leaders, the transformative leader is eager to learn not only from those who teach her but also from those she teaches. Mary Parker Follet avers that covenantal leaders (and in this case, transformative leaders who adopt covenantal leadership strategies) exercise "power with" rather than "power over" others. The application of all lessons learned, regardless of the source, that is in keeping with commands of God allow for innovative thinking and doing, "outside the box." At their best, the outcomes are exhilarating, even energizing, as all involved, teacher and learner, witness their gifts and graces to make room for their service to the advance of God's reigndom.

In summary, within the context of the Church, God sets the transformative leader in place to guide others along the journey to a more excellent way. At every step, such a leader is duty-bound to seek God for the vision, to aptly articulate the vision, and then to see God's vision through to fruition; all the while seeing those she leads valued as ends in themselves rather than a means to an end. A hands-on guide, who genuinely cares for those she both nurtures and teaches, the transformative leader is tireless and tenacious. The transformative leader is inspired as she inspires others, buoyed by the assurance that when and where the reigndom of God is advanced, renewal of minds results in their transformation. No one will leave the way they came in Jesus' name.

LEADERSHIP PRINCIPLES THAT WORK
Focus: A Key Component of Leadership

Meditation/Sermon
Fran T. Cary

Luke 9:57-62 (NRSV)

Introduction

As I age ever so gracefully, I notice that the most routine experiences of life contain new nuances that never existed in my earlier years. As a young adult, the mundane practice of having my blood pressure taken during a medical exam was inconsequential. However, at this stage of my life, the mere thought of the procedure can cause the numbers to soar. I can also remember when I possessed the ability to see the manufacturer's logo on the eye chart during my annual vision exam. Now, I find myself concentrating on the letters, giving thought to that to which I previously only glanced.

The latter example came to mind as I read the selected text. Many Biblical Versions list the passage under the heading, "The Cost of Following Jesus." Yet, the Holy Spirit invited me to not only glance, but ponder the passage. After further examination, I realized that the message was not merely directed to those walking with Christ. There is a poignant message to Christian leaders as well. The ability to remain focused on leadership is tantamount to success.

I. Be a Focused Follower

The ninth chapter of Luke begins with Jesus empowering the Twelve original disciples for ministry. He gives them specific instructions, and the text notes that they set out on their mission. They not only share the gospel but heal as well. As the reader proceeds, however, through the writing, the proclivities and mindsets were shown as well. They seem to display selfishness and agitation as they are not able to meet the logistical needs of the people. On the Mount of Transfiguration, an emboldened Peter appears to practice polytheism as he thought it wise to worship Moses and Elijah along with Jesus. Although previously anointed, they are now powerless against certain demonic spirits. Jesus calls them "faithless and perverse," He appears to be exasperated with their lack of execution. When Jesus spoke of his impending death, the author states that they were "afraid" to seek clarity on the matter. Instead, they begin arguing about who was the greatest of their group, and John wanted to rebuke other disciples who were not a part of their group (denomination), although they were doing the same. Although Jesus told them what to do when a group refused their ministry, James and John felt that the Samaritans who did the same should be killed by fire. Again, they were scolded by Jesus.

Someone outside the original group vowed that they would follow Jesus wherever he went. He informed them that this journey was no cakewalk, and when called another person answered with conditions.

Although this list comes from only one chapter, notice the thoughts and actions of those called by Christ. Directives given in the beginning were soon eclipsed by attention to other people, idolatry, fear, and self-aggrandizement. In other words, they lost focus as followers.

One may ask, what does this have to do with leadership? I am so glad you asked. One's methods and practices as a follower are the litmus test for their leadership ability. If **you cannot be a focused follower, you will never be a focused leader.** Leadership skills are not formed after one assumes a position; they are developed as a follower. A lazy follower will be a lazy leader. An undisciplined follower can only be an undisciplined leader. Our change in station does not transform one's character traits.

II. Focus for Accountability

Again, I note that this is not a passage to which one should merely glance. Most of those with whom Jesus spoke were avid students or disciples of his teachings. They were in the Master's class but unaware of the ultimate lesson. Jesus was training them for leadership. He knew that he would leave, and the Church would be established. Hence, his words were meant to prepare them for the greater, which was to come.

Twice in our selected text, Jesus spoke of the Kingdom of God. His true message superseded the quarrels and antics of the disciples. The Kingdom is centered around love, hope, and order. Therefore, they were being prepared for Kingdom work to which their sector would be the Church. Please notice that just as there is an order or even a hierarchy in the Kingdom, the structure must also be followed in the Church.

Our denomination, like many others in Christendom, is labeled as "Episcopal." This term references the governing oversight of leaders. While others may have differing views, I see this as a direct representation of our Lord, for it was he who took on the form of not only a follower but a slave. The way one follows parlays into the way in which they lead.

Notice that everyone happily begins as a follower. When we heed the prompting of the Holy Spirit and give our lives to Christ, we have no problem with our stage of infancy in the family. However, as we mature, we tend to look to a time when we can be in charge, making decisions, and instituting the policies. And, all of that may happen. However, the key is to remain a follower.

Every Pastor in the African Methodist Episcopal Church needs a Presiding Elder. Each Presiding Elder needs a Bishop. Bishops need peer support for accountability. For the few that will rise to the level of Presiding Prelate, the focus must not be lost. Decisions and judgments must be made for the advancement of the Kingdom rather than individual interest. The Scripture is clear in saying, "Where there is no guidance, a nation falls..." (Proverbs 11:14). No matter how far you advance, it is imperative that you never lose the heart of a servant.

III. Focus on the Kingdom

It is odd that of all the ways that this chapter could end, it concludes with a shocking analogy from Jesus. After all the bantering among the disciples, their criticism of those who were not like them, and the excuses presented by others, Jesus says, "No one who puts a hand to the plow and looks back is fit for the kingdom of God." Wait, who was talking about agriculture? Where did that come from?

Although the statement was directed at one person, it is applicable to all. The plower is in charge. The animals which pull the device are guided by the one behind the plow. The one who directs determines how the animals move, how straight the rows are, and ultimately how soon the work will be complete. Additionally, it is the plower who sows the seed, also known to us as the Word of God.

This role of leadership is of utmost importance. But one is not trained on the day they get the plow. They do not learn how to maneuver the livestock the moment that they get the bag of seeds. More than likely, training began by serving in the family, performing seemingly menial chores.

If one puts their hand to the plow and looks back or loses FOCUS, they can destroy work that has already been done. If one is not focused, she or he will not notice the need for the livestock to be refreshed. If one loses focus, he or she may furrow a row twice, uprooting what has been sown.

Clearly, Jesus says that if one cannot remain focused, they are unfit to lead. How odd that in our society, we label children with attention deficit disorder. Doctors are quick to prescribe medication that will help them to center and gain direction. We cannot afford spiritual ADD. Jesus was determined. As a matter of fact, he was so resolute in his mission that he had set all his intentions on going to Jerusalem as his time was at hand.

We cannot afford to lose sight because the mission is great. We cannot pray, "Your Kingdom Come...," and not be prepared to contribute to its preparation. For the Kingdom to be ready, we, as individuals, must be poised to work. We must have insight into unforeseen issues yet be willing to seek counsel (Matthew 6:10).

Conclusion

Messages such as this are intended to realign us. We all need this from time to time because we get so busy working that we fail to realize when our furrows are crooked. We become so entangled in work that we fail to remain accountable to others and seek wisdom from those who have plowed many a row before.

I admonish each of you to make time for reflection. Verify that you are in the place that God appointed you and that your motives for said work remain pure. There is a great day of reward coming. Do all that you can to be found faithful. Therefore, my beloved, "be steadfast, immovable, always excelling in the work of the Lord, because you know that in the Lord your labor is not in vain" (1 Corinthians 15:58).

CHAPTER 3

Excellence in What You Do

"Don't give it five minutes if you are not going to give it five years."
Meghan Markle

WHO IS THE GREATEST?

Meditation/Sermon

Janet Sturdivant

Mark 10:35-45 NRSV

35 James and John, the sons of Zebedee, came forward to him and said to him, "Teacher, we want you to do for us whatever we ask of you." **36** And he said to them, "What is it you want me to do for you?" **37** And they said to him, "Grant us to sit, one at your right hand and one at your left, in your glory." **38** But Jesus said to them, " You do not know what you are asking. Are you able to drink the cup that I drink, or be baptized with the baptism that I am baptized with?" **39** They replied, "We are able." Then Jesus said to them, "The cup that I drink you will drink; and with the baptism with which I am baptized, you will be baptized; **40** but to sit at my right hand or at my left is not mine to grant, but it is for those for whom it has been prepared." **41** When the ten heard this, they began to be angry with James and John. **42** So Jesus called them and said to them, "You know that among the Gentiles those whom they recognize as their rulers lord it over them, and their great ones are tyrants over them **43** But it is not so among you; but whoever wishes to become great among you must be your servant, **44** and whoever wishes to be first among you must be slave of all. **45** For the Son of Man came not to be served but to serve and to give his life a ransom for many."

Who is the greatest? Who is the one who stands head and shoulders above the rest? Who is the one who has distinguished him/herself as a per son to emulate? According to Webster's dictionary, the greatest is one who is prominent, eminent, important, renowned, famous, or well known. An individual who has accomplished what others only wish they could. The greatest is the one who has superior ability or skill in their field of study or occupation. In boxing, was Muhammad Ali the greatest fighter of all time? According to him, he was. The question is asked every basketball season, is Michael Jordan or is LeBron James, the greatest basketball player? Is Billie Jean King or Serena Williams, the greatest female tennis player? Is Tom Brady the best quarterback of all time? For now, these questions are great for conversation around the dinner table, and only time will answer who is or who isn't; but I still ask, who is the greatest? How can we judge what factors or traits should we look for in answering the question of who is the greatest?

Civil rights activist Dorothy Height said, "Greatness is not measured by what a man or woman accomplishes, but by the opposition he or she has overcome to reach his goals." Oprah Winfrey says, "Failure is another steppingstone to greatness." Martin Luther King, Jr. said, "Everybody can be great because everybody can serve. You don't have to have a college degree to serve. You don't have to make your subject and verb agree to serve. You don't have to know about Plato and Aristotle to serve. You don't have to know Einstein's theory of relativity to serve. You don't have to know the second theory of thermodynamics in physics to serve. You only need a heart full of grace, a soul generated by love." But Jesus simply says, "whoever wishes to become great among you must be your servant..."

In our text today, Jesus is on his way to Jerusalem, with a crowd accompanying him. However, on the way, Jesus pulls the Twelve aside and begins once again to share with them some of the events that are sure to occur once he makes it to Jerusalem. Jesus does not want them to be surprised by what's about to happen. Along the way, from time to time, Jesus has alluded to these events. He wants them to be prepared because the next few days will not be easy for them. They will see things they have never seen before and hear things they have never heard before.

They will find themselves without him, an experience they have not had since the first day they began following him. Certainly, there were times he was off praying, and they had to look for him, or he sent them in one direction only to meet them later that evening, walking on water. But the events that are soon to come they had never experienced before. However, the truth of the matter is they did not understand what Jesus was saying; **they heard his words, but they did not comprehend what Jesus was saying.** Evidenced by the fact that the showdown in the garden caused all to scatter except Peter and John. Even though Peter lingered, he still denied knowing Jesus! The rest of the disciples were nowhere to be found.

It was after this conversation, a time when Jesus expressed with great care what will happen in Jerusalem, the Bible says that James and John said to Jesus, "Can we ask you a question?" I do have a problem with the timing of their question, for to me, it seems as if they just skipped over the importance of that intimate moment. They are out of touch with Jesus; unfortunately, this is nothing new for the disciples. It was a selfish moment for them, but a sacrificial moment for Jesus. I had a problem with the timing at first, but I did not have a problem with the question. I felt these men had seen Jesus bless strangers. Jesus freely blessed and healed them, cast demons out of them, ministered to them, and even raised one from the dead. So why is it strange if they are in his inner circle? Can they not ask for whatever they want? After all, they gave up everything to follow Jesus. Some scholars suggest they were Jesus' relatives; that's why they asked. Some suggest it was just a selfish question to ask. But as I pondered the text, their father's name *Zebedee* became like a neon sign to me. In most of the Scriptures where James and John are mentioned, their names are preceded by the phrase *sons of Zebedee.* Who is Zebedee, and what could his name mean to this text? Their father was a fisherman who did pretty good for himself. The family had wealth signaled by the fact that they had hired servants. Their mother also followed Jesus closely. She is identified as one of the women who observed the crucifixion from afar, and she was one of the women who early Sunday morning went to the grave to anoint the Lord's body with spices. I believe this information suggests that James and John were well off and, therefore, could have been asking from a sense of entitlement. Maybe whatever they asked their father for they received, or whatever they asked their mother for they received. The Gospel of Matthew 20:21 records the mother requested special seating of James and John to Jesus on their behalf.

Oftentimes, the same attitudes and behaviors we have in the world are brought into the Church. The entitlements we receive in the world are what we feel entitled to in the Church. When you read the question in the backdrop of entitlement, it makes sense, and they wanted Jesus to do for them whatever they wanted. I know it is unnerving that they dared to ask Jesus to do for them whatever they wanted. But aren't we guilty of the same thing from time to time? Asking Jesus to bless us when we have no intention of being faithful over the blessing, we receive, for example:

- Lord, I want you to bless me financially; while I rob you of your tithes and offerings,
- Lord, I want you to make this man or woman love me even though they aren't saved, and I am,
- Lord, I want you to heal my body of this preventable disease or illness while I continue eating or drinking whatever I want and dis regarding sound medical advice,
- Lord, I want you to give me a million dollars; I want you to get me out of debt even though I blow every dime I get,
- Lord, I want you to promote me because I think I deserve the position never mind my evaluations they just hate me cause I'm cute or handsome.

And the list goes on, so you see James and John were not much different than we are today. Jesus said, what is it that you want me to do for you? What is it that you want from me, ask it? They replied, "Grant us to sit, one at your right hand and one at your left, in your glory." What they are asking is, Jesus, when you are sitting in the place where you are finally recognized as King; when you take over the Kingdom you have been teaching us about, we want the best seats in the house. These seats were considered seats of great importance. Only the most important people occupied the right and left side seats of the guest of honor. "The right was the most important, and the left was the second most important seat." They are not trying to be Jesus. They had sense enough to know he is the greatest; however, if they are just seen near him, they will get some recognition as well. Sometimes people hang with you because of who you are, not because they love you or even like you. But your position makes them feel important. ***Be careful who is carrying your water, that they are truly sensing and not seeking.*** I am not sure if James and John would have fought over which one of them would sit on the right or the left, or if they would sit according to their birth (the eldest sit on the right and the younger on the left)... you know how we do, always lining up our seating arrangements according to seniority or maybe they would have cast lots to determine who will sit where. Surely, they wanted these seats, and they had no regard for the other ten disciples. ***Selfishness never does think of others, but greatness is only attained by thinking of others.*** This request focuses not only on sitting on the right and the left but making sure it is at the right time when you come into ***your glory.*** Why didn't they ask to be seated with him during the suffering he had just explained he was going to experience? No, Jesus, we want to sit with you when the suffering is all over. When there is no price to pay to be with you, a time when life is good, this is when we want to be by your side. We see it often in the church of God, where members will have nothing to do with praying, planning, or preparing for that special day or celebration, but on that day, they are front and center. The members will not sacrifice and stay while the church is going through the building process, they cannot hang in there during the genesis of a ministry, or contribute to the capital campaign to finance the needed repairs to the building, but when it is time to march in the new building or claim membership as a member of the now thriving ministry or take credit for how good things look in the church they act and sound like they were never MIA. Only when the cameras are on, or names get called, certificates are given out or honors extended do some of these members show up at the church.

The one thing I know is, "If you ask, it shall be given if you seek, you shall find, and if you knock, the door will be opend to you." They asked, and Jesus answered, "You do not know what you are asking. Are you able to drink the cup that I drink or be baptized with the baptism that I am baptized with?" What cup was Jesus talking about? When Jesus was in the garden of Gethsemane, Jesus said: "My Father, if it is possible, let this cup pass from me." What cup was he speaking of, I believe it was a cup full of:

- Suffering
- Betrayal
- Denial
- Pain
- Rejection
- Abuse
- Loneliness
- Mocking
- Whipping

- Sacrifice
- Death

Jesus asked, "Are you able to drink the cup that I drink or be baptized with the baptism that I am baptized with?" What Jesus asked was, are they willing to die for the sake of the Kingdom of God? This was not water baptism Jesus was speaking of but his suffering and his ultimate death. Nevertheless, James and John had only seen the crowds running after Jesus; they had only seen the praise of Jesus by people; people were always seeking him out wanting to be around him; surely, Jesus, we can drink from the cup. *Once again, they heard what he said, but they did not know what Jesus meant.* It is easy to hear what God says or asks, and without even thinking, we say *yes, Lord*! Because we love God, and we know God loves us. So, we do not want to say no. It is not until we realize the cost of that yes, that we wonder, God, did I really sign up for all of this? Recording artist Shekinah Glory recorded t h e song, "Say Yes!" Some of the lyrics are, "Now, will your heart and soul say yes? Will your Spirit still say yes, yes? If I told you what I really need, will your heart and soul say yes?" The question God asks is often much deeper than we comprehend, and it was in the case of James and John. Even with them saying yes, Jesus responded: "The cup that I drink you will drink; and with the baptism with which I am baptized, you will be baptized; but to sit at my right hand or at my left is not mine to grant, but it is for those for whom it has been prepared." You see, James and John were both under the same illusion that many saints are today; when they see where you live and see what you drive. When they see how God has blessed you and when they see how you have been elevated by the Lord, *what they fail to realize is they might see your glory, but they do not know your story.*

- They have no idea all the hell you went through just to get to where you are today.

- They do not know the haters in your life, who, if they had their way today, you would not even be where you are, doing what you do.
- They do not know the meals you gave up, not because you were fasting, but you had no money to eat. The dresses and shoes you did not buy, the cars and suits you denied yourself of just to take care of your family.
- They do not know the nights you cried, the problems and tests you failed, the lies that were told on you, the persecution you endured.

Furthermore, the reason they do not know is that you do not look like what you have been through. James and John quickly answered, "We are able." Their answer reminds me of a politician who was vetted as a running mate for a presidential candidate a few years ago. She said when they asked her if she would run, she did not hesitate, she just answered yes. Oh, how I wish she had. Because she, like James and John, felt they were able, none of them were, and we are only able by the grace of God. Surely, they thought they were able because:

- They never saw the cross,
- They never saw Pilate's hall,
- They never saw Herod's court,
- They never saw the road to Golgotha,
- They never saw the crown of thorns,
- They never saw the lashes on his back,
- They never saw the choice between Jesus and Barabbas,
- They never heard Peter's denial or Judas' betrayal,
- They never saw the tomb, so sure they could drink the cup, for they did not see the cost of greatness.

Before we want to walk in someone else's shoes, we need to make sure we can fit them. But the focus of the text is not about seats or seating arrangements; it is about the discussion that is about to take place between Jesus and the twelve, **who is the greatest?** You see, just like some saints today, the disciples were confused by greatness in the Kingdom of God and greatness in the world. James and John felt as some saints do today: that if you are great, you are to be served. You are to be honored because you are special, set apart from everybody else. Not sanctified, set apart, but exceptions are made for you; your name is great; you are famous, a celebrity, so to speak. I call it being a church star. If you are great, you get the best seat in the house. You are ushered to the front for all to see. You are on the VIP list, and you are entitled to things others are not. Unfortunately, since we were born to worship, some of these VIPs want to receive the worship only God deserves. Please do not get me wrong, I do not hate those for whom honor is due.

As a leader in the church, I get ushered to the front, and I am seated at the head table, my name is called in the protocol. ***However, if I begin to think that all of this attention gives me value, then I have forgotten that a truly great person is the one who serves.*** For God alone deserves the glory and the honor. Jesus said, "The greatest in the kingdom of God is the one who is the servant of all." All the things that make people great and special in the world are not things that impress God. God is not interested in whom we think we are or what we think we have. God is not interested in whom people think we are or what they think we have. God does not get excited by us because God knows we can do nothing without him, and it is in him; we live and move and have our being. Jesus said it this way, "I am the vine; you are the branches. Those who abide in me, and I in them bear much fruit because apart from me, you can do nothing" (John 15:5).

The disciples by now (I am sure) were quite upset with James and John for asking this question. They may have even been ready to fight. Peter was boiling; after all, he was their spokesperson, their self-proclaimed leader, and if anyone deserved a seat, it was him. What if Jesus had granted their request that would have left the rest of them out? **But Jesus' point was missed; greatness is not about where you sit; greatness is about how you serve.** As Martin Luther King, Jr. said, "Anyone can be great because anyone can serve." This is the way of the Kingdom of God; Jesus did not come to be served, but he came to serve. If they are going to be great, they cannot do it the way the Gentiles do, but the way Jesus taught. They must be a servant of all. In the Kingdom, it is not about them, and it is not about us, it is truly a life of sacrifice for the Kingdom of God. People may never notice what you do, they may never say thank you, they may never call your name, they may never acknowledge your sacrifice, and they may never give you a promotion, but this is the way of the Kingdom. You can rest assured the road to greatness will be a lonely, narrow one. You can be misunderstood, misinterpreted, misquoted, overlooked, and missed altogether as if you are invisible. Greatness is giving with no promise of getting back. Although humankind may overlook you or disregard you, the joy in service is that God will pay you. After all, you are working for his glory. Pay is not always in the future. some of the rewards we reap right here, right now. And can I tell you God pays and the pay is good? In fact, it is said God is good all the time, and all the time, God is good.

So, do you have to pass a card out everywhere you go? Do you have to hear your name called at every meeting in the protocol? Can you do it without anyone knowing it was done by you? Can you let credit be given to someone else for something both of you know you did? **This is when you know you are a true servant; when what gets done is more important than your need to be acknowledged for doing it.**

The greatest example of a servant was the one who consulted with

God one day and asked for a body that he might come down and save the world. So, Jesus left his glorious kingdom and came down through 42 generations. He was born to a virgin, lived among his own, and his own received him not. He was born in a manger, in a barn, among stinky, dirty animals for there was no room for him in the Inn. He grew up and went about teaching, preaching, praying, praising, healing, and delivering, all for the Kingdom of God because he was a servant. If anyone deserved to be served, it was Jesus. Yet, one Friday on Golgotha's hill after he was whipped, spit on, mocked, persecuted, rejected, and nailed to the cross, he hung there while being challenged to come down and save himself, but Jesus was a servant. While being insulted by one who hung on his left side, he hung there till he died. Jesus hung there for all who believe; Jesus died there for all who believe; Jesus was pierced in the side there for all who believe, and Jesus laid there in a borrowed tomb for all who believe. He laid there all Friday night, he laid there Saturday morning, he laid there Saturday afternoon, he laid there Saturday night, but early Sunday morning, Jesus rose from the dead for all who believe. Jesus rose with all power in his hands. And when Jesus got up, we got up. Jesus rose as the greatest because he is the servant of all.

Who is the greatest, whoever is a servant!

CHAPTER 4

Living Beyond Ministry or Leadership in Your Personal Life
(Having a Life Outside the life of the Church

"Good or bad, strong or weak, large or small, you can or can't."
annehenningbyfield

"It is not what you look at that matters,
It is what you see."

Thoreau

LIVING BEYOND MINISTRY

Meditation/Sermon

Margaret Fadehan

The word "ministry," commonly referred to as *diakonia* in the New Testament, has been associated with a great variety of meanings. This meaning includes discipleship in general, as found in John 12:26. Ministry services are rendered to the church through gifts, the ministry of the Word, and feeding the poor and serving the community. Living Beyond Ministry encourages discussions from an early Sunday morning School of Ministry at my home church, which taught what it would entail living beyond fundamental descriptions of ministry.

One key task is to define what is the ministry, not just in terms of a dictionary or theological definitions, but in practical everyday ways. This is an important first task for the youth and young adult class for whom faith is not about ecclesiastical words and semantics, but about confronting real everyday issues and challenges, and finding the meaning of life.

One important conclusion about what ministry is: loving God and responding to God's ministry to each of us through God's Son, Jesus Christ. This conclusion, I would refer to as the first dimension of ministry. John 3:16 captures the crux of this first and crucial dimension, "For God so loved the world that he gave his only Son, so that everyone who believes in him may not perish but may have eternal life."

Thus, the ministry is first about God reaching out to each one of us, so that each of us may have eternal life. This ministry of God through God's Son ensures that the power diminishes everything that is at variance with God in our lives. We cannot claim to be one with God and yet remain in conflict with God in our thoughts, speech, attitudes, behavior, and lifestyle. If the Spirit of him who raised Jesus from the dead dwells in you, he who raised Christ from the dead will give life to your mortal bodies also through his Spirit that dwells in you. For if you live according to the flesh, you will die; but if by the Spirit you put to death the deeds of the body, you will live (Romans 8:11-13). God's work in each of us through God's Holy Spirit is first and foremost to conform and transform us into God's eternal image; to become like God, in love, righteousness, and power.

God: divine power has given us everything needed for life and godliness, through the knowledge of the One who called us by God's glory and goodness. Thus, God has given us, through these things, his precious and very great promises, so that through them you may escape from the corruption that is in the world because of lust and may become participants of the divine nature.

The ministry of God is about a life-changing experience, whereby old ways of living give way for a new way of living. It is a shift on the inside and the outside, and the task of a lifetime. It only culminates when we are translated from this world to the eternal.

Secondly, the ministry is about God working through us to minister to other people. Each of us is conduits to reach others with whatever God has for them. It helps us to understand that the gifts we have been given are not for our selfish plans and ambitions. Psalm 1:1-3 captures that picture in its allegorical comparison of people who have allowed God's Word to permeate their mind, soul, and spirit to fruit-bearing plants planted by streams of water.

God works in us, bringing about a transformation on the inside, which manifests on the outside in the fruit we bear. "Fruit" generally attends to a wide range of needs including food to provide strength, aid growth and development by helping the body to repair itself. The fruit we bear should minister to the various needs of people around us, whether formally or informally.

The third verse refers to the fruit coming forth in season, and a direct reference to timing and situational relevance. God's ministry working through us is designed for the appropriate time for the right situation. The word, the counsel, support, and whatever gifting we have received from God are meant to reach and touch the people and situations that need it. Holding positions of ministry are meant to be for a season, which God defines. The leaves will not wither, and there will be a prosperity of everything that we do.

From the previous, understanding living beyond ministry becomes clearer. God's ministry through us, particularly in formal contexts, has a defined time and place, the other is eternal. We can never live beyond God's ministry in us. It is a lifetime venture. There is never a time when we can afford to live beyond and without God's work in us. God's ministry to us and in us is what provides the grace and strength that we need to breathe, live, and to be able to exit this temporal world successfully, with an assurance of a better world beyond this earth.

In contrast, our ministry to others, the second dimension of ministry, is defined by time and place. This aspect of ministry is dictated by the seasons of life and our relevance in the eyes of God for his purposes at different points in time. Interestingly, while this aspect of ministry may certainly have peaks and dips, we can also say it certainly never ends completely. Formal positions of ministry often have a defined tenure, and our informal relevance to people and situations may peak at a point and diminish at another. However, we still find that till and in death, our lives and stories continue to make meaning and may provide inspiration or lessons for others.

Many despair when a season of life is over, mourning over the loss of relevance. Some even attempt to hold onto positions and circumstances when they ought to let go. Such attitudes only breed pain, hurt, and lots of discord. Sensitivity to the Holy Spirit is critical in such times. It is important to be able to identify when a season is over, and we need to move on. Ensuring that God's ministry in us continues unhindered enables us to identify and ascertain such times. Just as trees use the off-season period to rejuvenate themselves for the next season of relevance, so also we must ensure that when our relevance in ministry diminishes, it should serve as a signal for a time of rejuvenation when we need to focus fully on the first dimension of ministry—God's ministry in us. This is a God-focused ministry time for pruning, discarding the old, and giving room for a coming forth of the "new leaves" required for the next season in our lives.

What do we need to do in such times? Such times require that we find ways to withdraw into God's presence to spend more time with the Spirit of God, to read and meditate on the Word of God, and to listen to the Holy Spirit. Retreats are significant at such times, be it personal or group-based. In a nutshell, we need to take concrete steps to move out of the spotlight and focus on self-care and rejuvenation as we allow God's immeasurable grace and power to work in our minds, souls, and spirit to refocus, heal, and prepare us for the next time and place where he will need us as vessels again.

CHAPTER 5

If a tree falls on your path, walk over it, around it or get a chain saw and cut it up.

annehenningbyfield

Leadership While Living in a Drought

"Leaders must be tough enough to fight, tender enough to cry, human enough to make mistakes, humble enough to admit them, strong enough to absorb the pain, and resilient enough to bounce back and keep on moving."

Jesse Jackson

LEADERSHIP WHILE LIVING IN A DROUGHT: ARMCHAIR MUSINGS

Principle

Elaine P. Gordon

Let me begin by stating, this is not intended to be a thesis or a treatise. These are a few reflections and nuggets from the heart of a leader.

Special thanks to the late Juanita Bedenbaugh and Mary E. Beadles, who were the first women to challenge me to answer the call to preach. Whenever called upon to pray or speak on the missionary journey, they would angle up to me with, "You know, you should just go ahead and get ordained." What they could not have known was that I was afraid. Afraid because answering the call meant I was risking my marriage. I was married to a man who frequently remarked, "If God calls anyone to preach in this house, he must be calling for a divorce." With three children to raise, I convinced myself that what God really wanted from me was an evangelist.

It was in the summer of 1988 that the Rev. Jessica Ingram would angle up to me with a stern look and utter, "Don't you dare compromise the call on your life. God has people out there who will never believe they can follow Christ until they see the possibility through you. Somebody's salvation is in your mouth." Those words haunted me. It was those words that gave me the courage to say, "**If I perish, I perish**" (Esther 4:16, NASB). That was on a Friday, and that Sunday, I made my way down the aisle, wobbly legs and all made eye contact with my Pastor husband and declared I had decided to say yes! That is when I first learned what it meant to live in a drought while leading others.

A drought is a metaphor for those places in your life where there is a shortage, a void, a lack, a dry place. Other synonyms include non-existence, unavailability, deficiency, and thirstiness. Your drought can be physical, emotional, financial, psychological, or spiritual. Beloved, I venture to say that before this life is over, each of us will experience drought at some level.

So, what do you do when you find yourself in a dry and thirsty place, when your spouse does not divorce you, but shuts you out—physically, emotionally? When there is a drought in your checkbook, you are drowning in educational debt, and your appointment is in Timbuctoo. The package is $50 weekly, maybe or when your loved one dies, and in the middle of your grief, the phone rings because a member's loved one is actively dying, and you are called to the bedside, what do you do? What do you do when you are overwhelmed when your life is in shambles, and it feels like your whole world is falling apart? So, tell me where is the good news?

The LORD will continually lead you; God will feed you even in parched regions. He will give you renewed strength, and you will be like a well-watered garden, like a spring that continually produces water (Isaiah 58:11).

Principle #1: Find an oasis in your desert place.

We have this command to love one another as ourselves. It makes no allowances for what is going on in our lives. As I live and observe, however, I am convinced we are most obedient. Without proper care and attention, there is the tendency to love others out of our deficiency, creating toxic environments, and leaving carnage in our path. If we are to lead in love even while living out of a desert place, we will surely need to find an oasis. I find mine in my relationship with Christ, whose patient and non-judgmental love bids me come and lament. There I can be fully transparent.

Prayers of lament follow a distinct pattern: (1) Call to God—an acknowledgment of Gods Sovereign Rule; (2) Lodge the complaint—state your case, your concern, and your issue; (3) Make your declaration of trust— "And yet, will I put my trust in You" (Psalm 53:3); (4) Cry for help (Holla!) and express confidence in God to deliver; and, (5) Praise God for answered prayer. I find that lamenting provides a healthy outlet for my true feelings, reinforcing faith in God to quench my thirsting soul. Refreshed, I can preach, teach, and encourage others from my "not yet" space. Refreshed, God's Word becomes the substance and evidence for what is hope for and yet unseen (Hebrews 11:1 para).

Principle #2: All water is not fit to drink.

In Genesis 26, the story is told about how the Philistines filled the wells of Abraham with dirt. Note, Isaac did not drink from the dirty water; he dug new wells. Understand that Philistines are alive and well. They are still busy slinging mud. Philistines are those people who allow you to feel comfortable when even you know you are dead wrong, people who reinforce, even encourage your poor behavior/judgment calls. Be careful you do not start sipping from their wells of negativity and self-destruction.

As Bishop Edgar Vann so aptly put it, we each need enemies for our dysfunction. We need people who recognize who we really are and what we really desire, people who will lead us to become whom we are destined to be.

Digging new wells may mean replacing some people in your life, people who know you're better than you've been settling for. You do not know where I might be, were it not for people like Mother Delores Kennedy Williams, who is known for her candid commentary. On occasion, I was the target of some mudslinging. Mother Delores let me rant and then interrupted me and simply said, "Everybody gets a turn. It is your turn now and thinks not too highly of yourself, and someone else will be on the front-page tomorrow." Alternatively, Bishop E. Anne Henning Byfield, who refused to let me wallow in anger and bitterness. She sent me to St. Stephens, Hanover, a congregation with fifteen members. While I met their needs, they watered me with love and encouragement. God used those people to restore my confidence, to stimu late my creative and innovative self. From there, Bishop would stay in my life, challenging me, fast-tracking me, opening doors for me. Today, those wonderful people are on my Presiding Elder District. I am still drinking from their well.

Principle #3: Leadership is not about rhetorical gymnastics.

The past thirty years have taught me many lessons. I have been through the valley of not enough and non-existent more times than I can count, or there is enough room to tell. Nevertheless, through it all, God and I have developed an amazing relationship. God has manifested in unbelievable ways. I wake up every morning grateful to be alive, grateful to be allowed the blessed privilege of serving others. I have also learned to recognize the signs of drought.

At each point along the way, there were signs it was time to move on. From St. Stephens, Hanover, the last church in the district to Ward Chapel, Peoria, the first church in the conference, God enabled me to serve well, make a full report, to report converts and accessions, to build relationships, and to make a community impact. But, I began to feel tired. I lost my enthusiasm. I felt restless. That year Rev. Dr. Anne Lightner Fuller would be the presenter at our Minister's Retreat. She would announce her early retirement. Someone asked how she knew it was time to retire. She said, "I did not feel like going to work anymore. The people started getting on my nerves. It started to feel more like work than ministry." The tears fell, and my spirit cried, "That is me." The people had not changed. They were the same wonderful, hard-working people. It was me. Moreover, I knew it was time to move on.

Beloved, change is not the worst thing that can happen. The beauty of the itineracy is that it allows opportunities for a fresh start, fresh fire, and fresh ideas. Never stay anywhere going through the motions, preaching what you yourself cannot feel, saying what you do not mean, most of all dreading to show up to serve. Leadership is about building, building transformative communities, creating hospitable, and just space for the healing and deliverance of God's people. When you can no longer do that, move on.

Move on to the next chapter, the next career path. There's always the next. Reverend Dr. Olu Brown of Impact Church warns against looking for something new. For as long as we live and breathe, there is the next. As image-bearers, we bear in our bodies the likeness of a creative God who bids us show forth that creative likeness by constantly recreating. The question is, What is next?

Today, I am serving in a space where I can apply all the experience and wisdom gained over the past thirty years. I get to work with the brightest minds in the district, to provide space for the development of new leadership, to mentor, and to watch God do the incredible in unlikely places. Moreover, just recently, at the young age of 71, I have entered the doctoral program. I am drinking from my best cup and waiting to see what is next!

CHAPTER 6

Principles I Wish I Knew Early in Ministry

"It isn't that deep... you are the leader. Paying attention to the little details is that deep."

annehenningbyfield

"Catch the foxes, the little foxes that ruin the vineyard for our vineyards are in bloom."

Solomon

PRINCIPLES I WISH I KNEW EARLIER IN MINISTRY
Principle

Rosalyn Coleman

Some certain requirements and principles identify good leaders; however, there are, I feel, additional Bible-based requirements or principals that further identify Christian or godly leaders. Godly leaders require a different set of principles: principles that demand that the leader lives, loves, learns, and leads in a manner that is suitable to and compatible with God's Holy Word. These principles may require time and maturity to become a natural part of the leader's daily practices.

Now that I can look back and review some of my earliest experiences as a Pastor and Presiding Elder, what are some of the principles that I wish I knew earlier in ministry?

Principle #1: Do not Take It Personally! 2 Chronicles 20: 15

He said, "Listen, all Judah and inhabitants of Jerusalem, and King Jehoshaphat: Thus says the LORD to you: 'Do not fear or be dismayed at this great multitude; for the battle is not yours but God's.'"

Many leaders have a difficult time with questions coming from others, especially in a large group setting. They often receive questions, comments, constructive criticisms, and even feedback as personal attacks. As a result, they cut off, avoid, ignore, and simply do not entertain discussions. These criticisms often lead to debilitating breakdowns in communication. Both the speaker(s) and the listener(s) often shut down. Leaders must understand: It is not about you; it is about the Lord!

What do you do when you meet with trouble in the way of duty? Jehoshaphat's kingdom was invaded by the Moabites, Ammonites, and the Meunites. He was outnumbered and distressed. What did he do? He took the pious course of action. Jehoshaphat fasted, prayed, and sought

God. He prayed that we are nothing without you. We are relying on you, God, to win this one. God gave him the assurance. They believed and accepted the assurance of God, and God did it! God gave defeat to their enemies. When it seems that the multitude is attacking us, we must do as Jehoshaphat did. We must trust God. It is not our battle. The cause is God's, and God will handle it. God will fight the battle. We must trust, believe, and walk-in faith.

Principle #2: Speak with Your Ears

Let the wise will hear and gain in learning, and the discerning acquire skill...
Proverbs 1:5

You must understand this, my beloved: let everyone be quick to listen, slow to speak, slow to anger... James 1:19

Is anybody listening? Underneath many of the criticisms, disagreements, discord, frustrations, resentments, and outbursts in meetings is the need to be heard and understood. Listen before you speak. Good leaders listen a lot. Good leaders listen to spoken and unspoken communications. Too often, leaders allow their personal trials to interfere with their ability to listen. Pinned up anger often leads to excessive talking and destructive behavior. Successful ministries are not built upon arguing our positions, defending our views, and pushing our opinions, but rather, they are built upon pastoral awareness and response to the needs of people. We cannot be aware of the needs of people if we are not listening. Effective leaders discipline themselves to be quick to listen attentively to hear the other side to gain understanding. In essence, effective communication (listening) protects against division, dissension, disunity, and discord in the body. Listening goes both ways. We need to listen to God and people. In fact, both leaders and followers will do well to listen. We help others when we listen, and we learn valuable lessons, as well. Learn to speak with your ears and your eyes. Speak, look, and listen with kindness. Be a good listener, not as a technique to influence someone else, but as a way to let God's Word "Do what it do!"

Principle #3: Walk the Talk

In the same way, let your light shine before others, so that they may see your good works and give glory to your Father in heaven. Matthew 5:16

Some years ago, while pastoring, I had dinner with the ministerial staff and a couple of members one Sunday afternoon, and, as usual, I picked up the tab. When we got to the counter, I realized that the server had miscounted. One tab was missing, so I said to the cashier, "One meal is missing from this check." After determining which meal was missing, I paid the check, and we all left the restaurant. Approximately ten years later, this preacher, who was now herself a Pastor, said to me, "I will never forget what you did when we went out to eat one Sunday." She continued, "When you got to the counter, you told the cashier that a meal was missing from the bill." She said, "I thought to myself: I would have paid that bill and walked out, calling it a blessing. Nevertheless, then later, I thought about it, and I had to admit that it was the right thing to do. I want to thank you for being a good example as my Pastor."

The sermon is for the preacher and the people, and the preacher must practice what s/he preaches. This raises the question: What difference does the sermon make in our lives? In the Sermon on the Mount, Jesus talks about things that need to be done. He wanted his disciples to understand what their duties were. You are the Salt of the earth and the Light of the World. The Sermon on the Mount was designed to guide and regulate our practice. The sermon is intended to help people to receive instructions from God. In everything, acknowledge God, and God shall direct your path. When you walk your talk, you inspire those who are watching to glorify God in their practice as well. Remember, our talking must be seen in our walking.

As compassionate and caring Godly leaders, we must understand that effective leadership is necessary for church and individual growth and development, as well as for obtaining and providing the resources and services needed for church growth. We must learn and grow spiritually as we mature in the church. We must remember the Kenyan Proverb: ***Leadership comes from God.***

Principles That I Wish I Had Known Early in Ministry
Meditation Sermon
Jacqueline Smith

As I look back through the years, I realize that there were some principles that I wish I had known early in my Ministry: The Blessings of Tithing, How to Overcome Brokenness, and Knowing That the Enemy Is Real!

The Blessings of Tithing: Often, we think and assume that everyone tithes or knows about tithing. I wish that I had known then the importance of giving ten percent of my earnings to God. I believed in giving and being a blessing to others, but when it came to giving God what was rightly due to God, I truly fell short. I was never taught about tithing. You might say, how could that be? It all depends on your family and their relationship with God and money. We are truly a product of what we learn in our home environment. I was touched by the same values of my family about giving to God and money until I was taught something different. It was through the personal study of the Word of God that I began to tap into the depth and the richness of God's knowledge!

I began experiencing the blessings and rewards of God as a Window Opener, according to Malachi 3:10: "Bring the full tithe into the storehouse, so that there may be food in my house, and thus put me to the test, says the LORD of hosts; see if I will not open the windows of heaven for you and pour down for you an overflowing blessing" (NRSV). Through this Scripture, we can see the provision (meat) that goes into God's House and that our life is opened to Heaven.

I Made These Commitments to the Lord
1. To always recognize God as my only source of Provision - Philippians 4:19

2. To be a Faithful Tither - Malachi 3:8-11; 2 Corinthians 9:6-7; Matthew 6:33
3. To be a Good Steward of what God has given me - Luke 16:10
4. To continue to be a blessing to others - 2 Corinthians 9:11

How to Overcome Our Brokenness!

Brokenness means to be crushed, defeated, dispirited, or dejected.

When my sister and I were younger, we were made to feel less worthy because of the thoughtless words and actions of others! We were ridiculed because some people thought that we didn't come from the right family, have a degree, or weren't daughters of somebody important in the community. We were crushed and broken. Brokenness hurts, and it comes in many forms: anxiety, insecurity, rejection, shame, emptiness, bitterness, perfectionism, unworthiness, and the like.

The spirit of insecurity, brokenness, and rejection entered us. We allowed the opinions of other people who also had insecurities and brokenness to affect our lives. We experienced healing through encouraging ourselves, standing on God's promises, and having an in-depth study of the Word of God. We believed what the Word of God said about us. We changed our perspective about how other people saw us, and we looked through the lens of Christ's love. Christ propelled us to move and accomplish our goals, dreams, and vision.

Jesus is the ultimate healer, heart mender, and the source of our strength! If you are broken, ask Jesus to heal your brokenness. God heals the brokenhearted and binds up their wounds (Psalm 147:3). Jesus is always present to treat our wounds and heal our grieving hearts. To overcome our brokenness, we must realize that we must be made whole by a power greater than ourselves, the power of God! "The LORD is near to the brokenhearted and saves the crushed in spirit" (Psalm 34:18).

Knowing That the Enemy Is Real!

Early in my ministry, I faced spiritual problems with people that exhibited inappropriate and erratic behaviors at inopportune times. Indeed, I discovered that there was demonic oppression behind their action. They were not aware of it, and neither was I. It was during these times of manifestations that I realized how unaware I was about the devices of the enemy, Satan. I discovered how cunning he was and how he used people to carry out his plans to destroy their lives. "The thief comes only to steal and kill and destroy" (dreams, marriages, ministries, relationships, and the like) "I came that they may have life and have it abundantly" (spiritual abundance)! (John 10:10).

Satan's primary tactic is to deceive us and to keep us away from God. He is the accuser of the Brethren (Revelation 12:10). Undoubtedly, Satan is a tempter; he tempted Jesus in the wilderness (Matthew 4:1-11). He tempts us (1 Corinthians 10:13). Satan is a slanderer; he attacked Job's character (Job 1-2), and Satan is a liar; the original father of lies (John 8:44). For the weapons of our warfare are not merely human, but they have divine power to destroy strongholds. We destroy arguments, and every proud obstacle raised up against the knowledge of God, and we take every thought captive to obey Christ (1 Corinthians 10:4-5). "Let God rise up, let his enemies be scattered; let those who hate him flee before him" (Psalms 68:1).

We Have Been Given Our Instructions!

Put on the whole armor of God! (Ephesians 6:10-18). Discipline yourselves! (1 Peter 5:8). Think about these things! (Philippians 4:8). We have our Fruit of Life! (Galatians 5:22-23).

As we continue to go forth in our ministries, remember, "Little children, you are from God, and have conquered them; for the one who is in you is greater than the one who is in the world" (1 John 4:4).

CHAPTER 7

Living a Ministry of Servant Leadership

"I have three precious things which I hold fast and prize.

The first is gentleness; the second is frugality; the third is humility, which keeps me from putting myself before others.
Be gentle, and you can be bold; be frugal, and you can be liberal; avoid putting yourself before others
and you can become a leader among men."

Lao-Tzu

LIVING A MINISTRY OF SERVANT LEADERSHIP

Principle

Integrity, Commitment, Listening, Personal Sacrifice, Faithfulness

Darlene Smith

My time and opportunity had finally come to fulfill the call of God and exercise the itinerant ministry for which I had previously vowed to follow. I had done well with the Board of Examiners, and I just knew I would turn the world upside down like the Disciples of Jesus had done after the Ascension. With the spirit of anxiousness, excitement, and filled with the joy of any aspiring servant of God ready to serve humankind, I listened to the Bishop during my ordination with intense hearing. From the depth of my heart, I was proud to say, "I will go where I am asked."

I stood at the altar with the other students, ready to be ordained, and listened to the Bishop say, "Take heed that the person whom you present unto us be apt and meet, by their godly conversation, to exercise their ministry duly to the honor of God and the edifying of the church." As I continued to listen to the Bishop, I heard so clearly the seriousness of what I was about to enter. He said, "And you have heard, co-laborers, of what dignity and how great importance this office is whereunto you are called. Moreover, now, again, we exhort you in the name of our Lord Jesus Christ, that you remember into how weighty an office you are called: that is, to be messengers, watchers of the flock, and stewards of the Lord; to teach amid this evil world, that they may be saved through Christ forever," I knew then that I would be a servant to the people for which I was called to serve. It did not take me long to realize that my work was beginning. My first pastoral assignment led me to travel approximately 138 miles one way. I had to travel with my two preteen children who did not want to leave their home church to follow me. At that time, I did not realize the sacrifices, commitments, and faithfulness required to minister to so few people in such a remote place. As I moved my way through the back hills of Tebbutts, Missouri, there was much to experience. There were streets, a gravel road, cattle feeding alongside the fence, a corner neighborhood, country grocery store, and a post office.

At the top of the hill was a one-room white church on a small gravel road. On the way to the church, I was able to touch the trees and brush. There was also a cemetery, and somewhat of a shed which housed the restrooms and an unattached kitchen to the church, and two red foxes living under the church.

When I saw the church which I was assigned, I knew that my responsibility was to serve and focus on the growth and well-being of this congregation and its surrounding community. There was a group of elderly people who loved the Lord and their church. It was a congregation of men and women who had served the Lord throughout their lifetime. Although they appeared to be twice my age, they allowed me to become their pastor and served them. It was then I realized a Servant Leader concept was paramount in my ministry. I had no desire to be served but to serve and was willing to go through personal sacrifices to meet the needs of my congregation. It was never about the one who leads, but the ones who are being led. These ten congregants were willing to accept the vision of their pastor; and motivated to be committed, love, and serve. While they were considered a small rural church, they worked as champions, and the church grew.

Jesus was a true example of a Servant Leader because he served humankind and helped them to realize their potential and making them better as a result of his witness. He performed miracles not to be seen or admired, not for self-gain or temporary recognition, not for money or fame, but simply to serve the people, he loved, and help those in need. As a result, he made the ultimate sacrifice for humankind. Today, people all over the world can see their way through their trials and tribulations in a storm because Jesus was a Servant Leader.

I have also learned that the key to a successful ministry is to hold near and dear one's integrity. Jesus tells us that the things that come out of someone's mouth originate in the heart (Matthew 15:8). A leader must be aware of their words for words are an indicator of the spiritual condition. Many of the lessons I learned from my mother, along with principles I developed later in life, such as honesty and sincerity. These lessons have always helped me to live an upright life, not a life not without flaws, challenges, mistakes, and/or failures, but obedience to God's voice. "And David shepherded them with the integrity of heart; with skillful hands, he led them" (Psalm 78:72). A leader must live a life of integrity and be an example for the ones they serve.

At each church, committed people were willing to serve the Lord no matter what. Commitment played a vital role in shaping my ministry. For example, each Sunday, I was met by the oldest member of the church who made the fire to keep the church warm. He was committed to seeing to it that the church was warm when we entered the church, a potbelly stove was blazing, and the embers seemed to have a prominent place. I always heard the popping and crackling sounds of its work to keep us warm. Brother Jack and Brother Pannell were eager to do their duty each Sunday morning wearing their bibbed striped coveralls and boots as they proudly served the Lord with their God-given gifts. They were also committed and exemplified that I equally must be as committed to a church and its congregants by serving them and helping them become all they can be in Christ.

Serving this church taught me that most of them only wanted a listening ear to share how they made it over and how God had given them just one more day. They saw new mercies each day and needed a Pastor who would listen, and I did not force my own view on them. I became the person they needed and wanted. Being a Servant Leader requires that you listened to people and do not force your views on them.

Together, we made a great team that was open to the voice and vision that God placed in our care.

My mission is to inspire and equip all for service. Jesus was the true example of serving others and empowering them and helping them to find their way. Jesus said in the Gospel according to Mark, "Jesus called them together and said, you know that those who are regarded as rulers of the Gentiles lord it over them, and their high officials exercise authority over them. Not so with you. Instead, whoever wants to become grand among you must be your servant, and whoever wants to be first must be a servant of all. For even the Son of Man did not come to be served, but to serve and to give his life as a ransom for many." Jesus led by example.

It is impossible to lead people without having a serious sense of devotion to God. The Scripture teaches us to pray without ceasing. Without prayer, it is impossible to move people in the direction in which God would have them to move. We must show the unbeliever the way of righteousness. We must be strong in the Lord and know that God is in control. God must be pleased with the Servant Leader of God. If you plan to walk with God, you must be filled with the power and presence of the Lord every day of your life. The life that we live requires that you maintain this intimate prayer life and depend and trust in God to the fullest.

As I think back to the first day of my pastoral, my first charge, I remembered the personal sacrifices I had to make (they are too numerous to mention). These sacrifices made me stronger as a pastor and prepared me for what was to come. I traveled for six years with three different assignments in approximately the same area, to a community waiting to serve and be served. I witnessed how God dressed the elements of nature and led me every step of the way. I learned that God does not make mistakes; just bloom where you are planted. You are to go where you are sent, and you are to make disciples for God's Kingdom. God's people are everywhere. Small congregations need a great pastor, and there are no little churches or big churches; it is all in one's mindset. You are what you aspire to be. As the songwriter wrote, "I'll go, I'll go, I'll go, I'll go, if the Lord wants somebody, here am I send me, send me." There are rewards in faithfulness!

LIVING A MINISTRY OF SERVANT LEADERSHIP

Meditation/Sermon
Carlene Sobers

Living a Ministry of Servant Leadership: A Call to Keep

St. John 13:1-12 (NRSV)

Earnestly, I sought for the voice of God to speak clearly to what God would have me to contribute towards encouraging God's people. How would the delivery of God's Word inspire us to be better leaders or to be "Servants" of the most high God?

Today, we know that regardless of who we are, we are impacted by our cultural background, or position of leadership title. It is revealed in Scripture that our titles mean nothing more than the mere fact that we have been called to serve as God served. Regardless of who we are socially or intellectually, or culturally, or position today, it must be in servanthood.

Jesus left us the perfect example of what it means to be a servant. This example went beyond his ordinary expressions of teaching by way of parables. He not only made himself to be a living sacrifice for us but also to be a living example of servanthood. We are given insight into what was an intimate occasion and the most delicate time as this led up to the final moments, which Jesus would spend with his disciples. He prepared himself to face the end of his earthly assignment, gathering his disciples for what would be the exchange of the ultimate teaching tool that would be a lasting impact on ministry. Jesus humbled himself to show that he was not only the Messiah but also a servant.

Jesus teaches us that while on divine assignment, there will be times when aspirations for service will lead us into lonely places, times of betrayal, and disappointments. However, we cannot back down, be afraid, or lose heart, but we must press forth in humility to accomplish the task knowing that Jesus loves us and will see us through to the end.

Jesus also reveals to us through God's Word that servanthood requires us to take off and leave behind that which would hinder us during our walk; we must put on the righteousness of God to fulfill our calling. Jesus took off his outer robe to gird himself with the towel to perform the task of washing the disciple's feet. He carried out the ritual of pouring the water into the basin and individually wash and dry each disciples' feet. This act was following the custom and tradition of their time and was done by the servant or the host of the house to welcome guests after their journey. It was not expected that Jesus the Messiah would perform such an act, nor was it about status, but rather it was an outward show of humility.

Likewise, the instruction to serve, therefore, should cause us to acknowledge that we all have a calling on our lives that has been designed by God. We have been assigned to a ministry. God has personally called, appointed, equipped, and empowered us to serve. The call is a clear call for servanthood. This call to the ministry specifically assigns us to serve God in specific areas to uplift God's house of worship and as caregivers of the community. Some have been assigned the call to be preachers, some teachers, some exhorters, apostles, prophets, evangelists, auxiliary leaders, missionary workers, and others to minister through expressions of worship in song and liturgical dance and other giftings. It is a clear call of commitment, a call that unites God's people to impact and transform lives. This is a call not just for us to hear and accept that God has called us; but rather, to pursue it, and move towards executing our calling with hope, determination, courage, strength, and focus to complete the mission assigned. In doing so, we must, however, be mindful that to be a leader, we must first master the art of being a servant. The call is not an individual self-call, but a wecall if we intend to make a difference and to have any kind of impact in the world.

As a member of the African Methodist Episcopal Church, we are cognizant of the fact that we are building on the foundation of a religious pyramid that has been founded for the right of freedom that all may carry out the mandate of God. We are called not only to hold fast to the legacy that has been left for us but also to continue determined. We must build upon the sweat, tears, and sacrifice that has been made before us for the sake of the Kingdom of God. We, therefore, are called under our vision to step out of self, to seek out, to save the lost, and to serve the needy. We must live out the purpose for which we have been established to make available God's biblical principles to the world. That is, to spread Christ's liberating gospel and to provide continuing programs that will enhance the social development of all people. We have work to do and a legacy to leave for generations to come that they may know Christ. The question is, "Where are we in our present service?"

It is evident in the overall analysis that as a people, we have fallen off in our pride, our passion, drive, and commitment. We have become too busy and too cluttered, even unbothered to be a real part of the service. We lack vision for life, the church, and the real things of God. We lose sight without realizing that we have placed God's purpose for the Church on life support, and the reality is that many churches are just barely surviving.

So many times, we take God for granted. We cease to be whom God designed us to be, and we cease to walk, talk, and operate in the way that God requires us to. We have allowed the struggle for power, the over-adoration of self, and the material things of life to become our gods, causing us to forget that our mandate is to serve others. But today, God speaks to the Church in urgency for us to rise up in unity, to march forth consistently, armored and equipped with God's Word to do battle against the enemy of our soul. Do you know what you were called to do?

- Are you able to recognize it?
- What is your response to God's call?
- Are you a contributor to the expansion of God's Kingdom?
- Are you willing to love as Jesus loved and serve as He served?

Conclusion

Brothers and sisters in this great Zion, we have a work to do; we have a call to keep; therefore, let us as God's people arise and serve. Let us hold fast to our calling and put aside anything that may hinder us from doing what God has established us to do. Let us serve in sincerity and truth.

The call to serve will not be easy, but if we acknowledge that we are God's people and the sheep of God's pasture, then we will know our loving Shepherd will protect us in this journey of life. Go Forth Living a Ministry of Servanthood and a Call to Keep!

CHAPTER 8

Balancing Compassionate Leadership

"After climbing a hill,

one only finds there are so many more hills to climb."

Nelson Mandela

A PRESIDING EIDER'S VIEW

Principle

Brenda Beckford Payne

Effective Christian Leadership is vital to the continued success of the Great Commission to "go, preach, teach, and make disciples." It is doubly important in this era of the Church where women again have assumed vital and challenging leadership roles.

Scope of Leadership

I have served the Church in leadership roles at varying levels, culminating in my current role as Presiding Elder. Leadership principles can be practiced regardless of position. Therefore, the keys and principles we learn and formulate in organizations, teams, and smaller contributions translate effectively to the pastorate, superintendence, and episcopacy. My leadership framework is based on observing great leaders in my Christian life and complementing the example they provided with my core values. Effective leadership sets a vision, elevates values, and guides the organization in the direction needed to accomplish the vision.

The Balancing Act

Leadership requires a person to be attentive to a plethora of concerns: rules, regulations, directives, duties, and responsibilities, policies, procedures, protocols, schedules, all of which need attention and care. One must have laser focus, be decisive, attentive to details, a game-changer, regulator, an evaluator, an enforcer, a disciplinarian, and careful of the limitations and extremes of such responsibilities. These responsibilities require the leader to be mindful of the limits and extremes of their leadership style that could derail their effort.

A heavy-handed approach might sabotage productivity, decrease morale, and result in incomplete assignments. A compassionate approach considers the personal dynamics of the ego, the psyche, and self-fulfillment that leads to a successful outcome. However, too much of an extreme compassionate approach yields the same negative outcome of a failed assignment.

A balance between the two is needed for church growth and the growth of each pastor and congregation. Can I be honest at this point? This balance is not always easily attainable. Personality and personal experiences mold us as human beings, then as leaders. Sometimes, one must work to improve oneself, and even change behavior, learn new approaches, and solicit mentors to coach and support us.

Personal Leadership Values

I am an only child raised by two wonderful parents. My values stem from my parent's meager beginnings, personal struggles with school bullies, and a professional team leading in nursing. My leadership style is deeply rooted in values such as kindness, compassion, and concern for the downtrodden, the underdog, the oppressed, and the distressed. Christian leadership must care for people—and even unlikeable people!

Christian leaders must have compassion. Our charges require strong shoulders and listening ears to hear their concerns with a mindset rooted in the Word and nurtured in our experience as women. Compassion also applies to leaders within our organizations. Developing a mindset of compassion within the organization enriches the response and effectiveness of the organization, which extends its appeal and draws new members who desire to affiliate with a positive place.

Christian leaders who demonstrate compassion provide godly concern for the work assigned to them. The world today demands so much from people in so many areas of their lives. A leader that is not concerned about how those demands affect his or her charges runs the risk of irrelevance, ineffectiveness, and abandonment by an underserved people. Compassion breeds concern about people that allows us to help, not hinder; instruct, not impede; guide, not govern; enlighten, not excoriate; enhance, not excuse; and encourage, not deter.

These personal leadership values allow me to provide servant, transformational, and instructional leadership. Jesus taught us that the leader is first and foremost a servant. We are not called to "lord it over" our charge, but rather to meet their needs through service. Jesus told us that no master is greater than his servant. We accomplish this by effective communication, listening as well as guiding, effective selection and delegation in team building, and removing obstacles to success. We serve the organization we lead rather than our organization serving us.

When the organization feels the impact of our exemplary service, it becomes easier to guide them into transformational leadership. Romans 12 reminds us to not conform to this world, but instead to be personally transformed. Persons in leadership can neither accept the *status quo* nor propagate it forever. We must lead with views towards transforming individual lives, team effectiveness, and organizational and congregational vitality. Each leader should approach each assignment with prayer, spiritual tools, and servant leadership principles to move on the path of renewal that God has for them.

Effective leaders instruct. Leaders must see where the organization or charge is and look for ways to apply Scripture, prayer, and guidance to create learning opportunities. Our Lord used parables to instruct Kingdom principles to his disciples so that the listening audience could understand. Leaders who provide instruction to their members, organizations, and charges in a variety of ways will enhance their understanding and transformation.

District Leadership Values

As a Presiding Elder and caring leader, I must invest in ministerial and lay leadership to foster church as well as personal growth. Using this framework of compassion and concern to achieve servant, transformational, and instructional leadership, I have developed for the South Houston

District (SHD) the theme "Soaring to Higher Dimensions," which is divided into five co-equal parts: Spiritual Enhancement, Evangelism and Outreach, Stewardship, Economic Development, and Leadership Training.

Spiritual Enhancement focuses on building and growing leadership, both individually and collectively. Effective leaders find plans and tools to enhance their understanding of the Word. This focus entails more effective communicants of the gospel. It enhances personal and corporate worship and elevates the framework of our liturgy and service through enhanced prayer, fasting, praise, preaching, and promise. When our charges are spiritually enhanced, numerical growth becomes an ancillary reward.

Congregations that are vibrant through enhanced personal commitment and understanding of the Word can become effective in evangelism and outreach. Our goal as transformational leaders is to help our charges see that church goes beyond "just our family—us four and no more." Transformational leaders must empower the membership to "break out" and go forth, meet and greet, reach out, and touch and share the Good News story. Then it is also possible to share their testimony with love and compassion. Leadership must care enough to place a higher priority on winning souls more than raising money.

Transformed congregations are more prone toward a stewardship-orientation. Effective vision, instruction, and guidance assist our congregants and members in understanding their financial role in the church. This role is one of the hardest challenges that leaders have because it is hard to communicate an understanding of wealth and power.

Effective stewardship leaders must convey a better understanding of how kingdom-building principles lead to love and concern for others. That good stewardship requires congregants and the leadership to man age our resources in such a way that giving becomes a joy and a desire, and not a burden.

This chapter has emphasized the importance of instruction. Leaders must identify ways to develop those persons that they must lead. Some tried and tested ways to train others are workshops, personalized study, group study, and team assignments that take organizations into challenge-specific settings. Nevertheless, look for new ways to prepare God's people to pray and ask God to reveal the strategies to you. The work of ministry cannot rest on the laurels of the past. Using technology could change the means of instruction to reach far beyond the face-to-face meeting at the church. Embrace every tool at your disposal to gain insight to help you become a genuinely caring, compassionate, transformational, and instructional servant leader.

CHAPTER 9

Learning from Failures

"Hard days are best because that's when champions are made."

Gabby Douglas

LEARNING FROM FAILURES

Principle

Linda Faye Thomas Martin

"Fail Forward"

PRINCIPLE 1 - Failing to Forgive

We, as Christians, must learn to be good at forgiving people because we will be doing it all our lives. When we forgive, we are doing ourselves a favor. We are freeing ourselves from the agony of anger and bitter thoughts. If we live, we will encounter people who hurt us, reject us, disappoint us, use the wrong tone of voice with us, fail to understand us, or let us down in the time of need. We must and need to take the high road and forgive!

Jesus knew the truth. That is why he responded as he did when Peter asked him: "Lord, how many times may my brother sin against me, and I forgive him and let it go? (As many as) up to seven times, but seventy times seven" (Matthew 18:21-22 NSRV)! What he meant was, "Forgive and keep on forgiving; Just keep on forgiving!"

PRINCIPLE 2 - Failing at Learning from Rejection

When people reject you, you may not want to keep doing what you are supposed to do; you may want to find a place to hide and nurse your wounds, but do not! Keep moving forward, no matter who or what disapproves of you, or tries to stop you.

If you look back throughout your life, you will probably find that every time God has tried to take you to a new level, the pain of rejection often causes you to abandon your determination to do what God has called you to do! Rejection causes us to convince ourselves we cannot do anything, especially in the Church. We are failures with a capital "F," and we need to remember that we may not please (Church) people, but if we please God, then that is all that matters!

Jesus dealt with the issue of rejection. In this passage, he warned His disciples that some people would reject them, and he told them how to handle that rejection. "And whoever will not receive and accept and welcome you nor listen to your message, as you leave that house or town, shake the dust (of it) from your feet" (v. 14) (Matthew 10:5-14). In a very real sense, they were to "SHAKE OFF" THE REJECTION and GO ON. You have two choices when you find yourself in this challenging circumstance: you can give up or go on.

PRINCIPLE 3 - Failure or Steppingstone

No one sets out to fail or wants to fail. I do believe "failure" can be an essential steppingstone on the way to success. Failure indeed teaches us what not to do, which is often as important as knowing what we are to do! So-called failure is all about how we look at it.

Many stories had circulated about how many times Thomas Edison failed before he invented the incandescent light bulb. It has been told that he tried seven hundred times, two thousand times, six thousand times, and ten thousand times, but he never gave up. Edison is reported to have said in all his efforts that he never failed—not once; he just had to go through many, many steps to get it right. It takes that kind of determination if you are really going to do anything worthwhile.

The man who led IBM had no fear of failure. In fact, he had this to say about it, "Would you like me to give you a formula for success? It is quite simple. Double your rate of failure. You are thinking of failure as the enemy to success. But it is not that at all. You can be discouraged by failure or learn from it. So, go ahead and make mistakes. Make all you can, because that is where you will find success."

CHAPTER 10

Finishing Strong

"Can a leopard change its spots?

No, but you can with ingenuity, creativity, hard work, and lots of paint!"

annehenningbyfield

"Nothing is too hard for you."

Jeremiah

FINISHING STRONG

Principle

Rosetta Swinton

A Leader After the Heart of God Is a Follower

In March 2017, *The New York Times* published an article written by Susan Cain in which she wrote, "In 1934, a young woman named Sara Pollard applied to Vassar College. In those days, parents were asked to fill out a questionnaire, and Sara's father described her, truthfully, as 'more a follower type than a leader.' The school accepted Sara, explaining that it had enough leaders." It is reported that the school replied, "Dear Applicant: A study of the application forms reveals that this year our college will have 1,452 new leaders. We are accepting you because we feel it is imperative that they have at least one follower."

In life, many people seek to have peace, love, joy, and happiness as an underlying desire for their day to day existence. Most people focus their attention on the needs they have for themselves, family, work, school, and social interests. In the daily process of life, people are still seeking something better because they believe that there must be something more to life on earth. At the same time, others are seeking something other than the things of this world. The search for answers is often sought from leaders in a variety of places, including the church. The answer to the question must do many times with one's heart. Leaders today in the church face a barrage of issues that impact families, communities, politics, nations, and the world.

This discussion will examine briefly how a leader after the heart of God serves anywhere to fulfill the calling of Jesus to make disciples by going and by teaching. "Whoever wants to be my disciple must deny themselves and take up their cross and follow me" (Luke 9:23 NRSV).

To be a good leader, one must first learn how to be a good follower. Sometimes leaders forget this basic instruction from Jesus to follow. Many leaders are consumed with being in control, but often forget that as they serve, they must always listen for and follow the direction of Jesus. As disciples of Jesus, leaders must be intentional in their role to follow Jesus as they lead others to do the same. Jesus explained to the disciples, "If any want to become my followers, let them deny themselves and take up their cross daily and follow me" (Luke 9:23).

Following Jesus means obeying the call to make disciples as he did. Matthew 28:16-20 represents a call to leaders into a worldwide ministry with the authority of Jesus to back them as they go. Jesus was very clear in what he expects from a disciple. A disciple must "go" where they were being sent is also clear. They are to "go" into all the world. "Go" is a very interesting word because to "go" *poreuthentes* means to depart, walk, go (one's) way (RSV), and requires action.

Leaders today are still called to copy the example Paul shared with his proteges Timothy and Titus in the early church, to fulfill the same qualifications in their personal life, church, community, and society as leaders are godly servants to God's people. No leader is perfect or free of making mistakes. This is an area that begs for attention in the lives of many spiritual leaders. True leaders are willing to admit first to themselves, confess to God, repent, and turn away from repetitious mistakes, take up their cross, and follow Jesus. When leaders are less than authentic in their own lives, the reflection in the mirror is like that of Peter, who denied Jesus three times. Jesus responded to Peter in love by forgiving him instead of casting him aside.

When God called me to go to Africa to serve in mission work for two years, I left everything I knew that was dear to me: family, friends, job, church ministry, and women's ministry to answer the call. I was given Matthew 28:16-28 as my scriptural foundation. I traveled to the

Republic of Malawi after God's heart was placed in me through a vision. I was instructed later that I would need God's great big heart in order to minister to the people I was sent to in Malawi. Daily, God was teaching me that obedience was better than sacrifice for almost a year before I received my new heart. Since being in Malawi for over ten years now, my great motivation was the reminder that the heart I had received from God was to be used to love, nurture, care, and minister to the people. I frequently had to shut down my old heart's way of thinking and to feel and obey the Holy Spirit, who guided me daily. The love I shared daily was God's love. The patience needed in many situations was God's patience. Although I had many good ideas, they were not God's ideas, and they did not always work. I came to learn that a leader makes mistakes more times than they realize, and the impact on others is a part of the choices and decisions made that will win someone to Christ or chase them away. God is love. "Beloved, let us love one another because love is from God; everyone who loves is born of God and knows God" (I John 4:7).

Leaders today are encouraged to clean up their lives and snap out of the mindset that causes them to feel that their place of influence and affluence makes them untouchable. Many leaders in the Church today are being exposed publicly for their secret behaviors that are unbecoming of a leader. With the help of the Holy Spirit, whatever their weakness, habit, or sinful ways, God can help them to be delivered and set free. Sin is not a respecter of religion, ethnicity, gender, or level of success. Sin can pull a leader from the very top, right down to the very bottom. Leaders must be very intentional to guard their hearts and "Take care, brothers and sisters, that none of you may have an evil, unbelieving heart that turns away from the living God" (Hebrews 3:12). The Apostle Paul declares, "Be imitators of me, as I am of Christ" (1 Corinthians 11:1). As one in the position of power, authority, influence, affluence, a leader is required to be an authentic example to the followers as they follow Christ.

A well-known author on leadership, John Maxwell, shares that "everything rises and falls on leadership" and reflects the potential power of a leader. A leader has the potential to build up or tear down the lives of followers. Jesus has lived the life model of the Good Shepherd, and authentic leaders should copy the same and be such a shepherd. But, Woe to the shepherds who destroy and scatter the sheep of my pasture! Says the Lord" (Jeremiah 23:1).

Making disciples is an essential and critical command in the life of those Jesus called to leadership positions (Matthew 28:19). It is, however, one that is buried beneath other programs, ministries, and creative ideas that are good, but not God's ideas. Nations around the world are riddled with poverty, corruption, syncretism, and immorality as followers of Christ are seemingly comfortable with entering the building to worship. Still, many do not leave to make disciples. There is a disconnect between the leader and the followers who are not being trained as disciples for them when leaving the worship experience, are then able to "go" and "make disciples." If one were to question leaders and followers in churches today about the number of disciples they have made, many would reply "none." Many followers believe that it is the sole duty of the pastor to "make disciples." But leaders must change that mindset by their followship to follow Jesus' command actively to make disciples. When the leader makes disciples, the followers will also make disciples.

For some time, after offering discipleship training at a church, I pastored in Blantyre, Malawi (Central Africa); the biggest challenge was getting more members to attend the training classes. The Holy Spirit led me to create a discipleship training program for the youth. I used the same adult guide but modified it for the youth and began teaching them to be disciples of Christ. Their excitement and enthusiasm were always high when we met each month for classes. After three months, I started taking them out with me to our already scheduled weekly evangelism outreach in the village and market in Blantyre, Malawi. At first, fear and timidity would overtake them. I would remind them and encourage them along the way, and one or two people would receive Christ after they shared their scriptural tract and words of encouragement (2 Timothy 1:7). I was always there, advising and championing them.

Soon, a six-year-old, although shy at first, when encouraged that her pastor was right there with her, was able to win five church-going people at a village brick making worksite to accept Jesus as their Lord and Savior. They admitted to attending a church regularly but had never accepted Jesus. Later, a thirteen-year-old knocking on doors in the village was able to share the good news with a group of eight Muslims, who said they had never heard of Jesus. Nonetheless, after telling the story of Jesus and sharing the salvation message, the eight Muslims accepted Christ as their Lord. While we were outreaching in the village at a primary school, a fifteen-year-old girl shared the good news of Jesus with children on a village playground, and twenty-one children believed the gospel message and accepted Jesus.

Leadership is not only for adults but also for the youth. God will use anyone available to win the lost and to make disciples. The call to make disciples must once again take precedence over other activities that the Church identifies as *doing church*. God is looking for leaders who will be the Church and make disciples. God is looking for leaders who will follow the command in Matthew 28:16-20. A leader must go, and a leader must make disciples, following the lead, guidance, and instructions of the Holy Spirit.

ABOUT THE CONTRIBUTING WRITERS

BISHOP E. ANNE HENNING BYFIELD serves as the 135th elected and consecrated Bishop of the African Methodist Episcopal Church serving in the 16th Episcopal District. Her historic election, in the year 2016, represents the first time in the history of the AME Church that a person was elected who had a sibling on the bench of Bishops, Bishop C. Garnett Henning, Sr.

She has received numerous awards including the Samuel DeWitt Proctor Beautiful Are Your Feet Award. She is the author of three books and numerous other printed and spoken word materials and musical compositions. Married to Ainsley for 43 years, they have one son, Michael, and four grandchildren.

THE RIGHT REVEREND CAROLYN TYLER GUIDRY is the retired 122nd elected and consecrated Bishop of the African Methodist Episcopal Church. Bishop Tyler Guidry is a lifelong AME member and the mother of two Itinerant Elders serving the AME church. She has two grandsons who have entered the ministry in the AME church. Bishop Tyler Guidry is the mother of five sons and one daughter, thirteen grandchildren, and eleven "great-grand."

PRESIDING ELDER DR. FRAN T. CARY presides over the Midwest North District in the Midwest Conference; Fifth Episcopal District. She is a General Board Member of the African Methodist Episcopal Church, Vice-Chair WIM General Board, Fifth District Women in Ministry Commissioner. Education: B.A. in Business Administration, MTS Central Baptist Theological Seminary.

THE REVEREND ROSALYN GRANT COLEMAN has served in the 7th Episcopal District as a Pastor for 17 years and a Presiding Elder for the past 22 years. She pre sides over the Columbia District of the Columbia Annual Conference. She was married to the late Reverend Melvin Coleman and has one daughter, Kristen Michelle Coleman.

THE REVEREND MARGARET FADEHAN currently serves as Presiding Elder of the Ife / Benin District of the Nigeria Annual Conference of the 14th Episcopal District, and District Women in Ministry President. She is also the Pastor of Christ Love AME Church, Ile - Ife, where she has established and expanded various outreach and sustainable empowerment programs and projects.

THE REVEREND MARILYN A. MILLER GILL serves as the second Executive Director of Indiana Christian Leadership Conference (formerly an affiliate of original Southern Christian Leadership Conference (1957)); associate minister at St John's Missionary Baptist Church, Indianapolis, IN. Education: BA, Leadership & Ministry and BS, Ethics & Management from The College of Biblical Studies, Indianapolis, IN; M. Div. from Indiana Wesleyan Seminary, Marion, IN; current doctoral student at Newburgh Theological Seminary, Newburgh, Indiana; and Honorary Doctoral Degree from Habakkuk Bible College, Indianapolis, IN.

THE REVEREND DR. ELAINE P. GORDON is the Presiding Elder of the South District, Indiana Annual Conference, Fourth Episcopal District of the African Methodist Episcopal Church. She is the second female Presiding Elder to serve in the Fourth Episcopal District.

A transplant from California, Reverend Gordon holds the Bachelor of Science degree in Social Services Administration, and the Master of Arts degree in Urban Ministry from Martin University. A lifelong learner, Rev Gordon is a student in the doctoral program at Payne Theological Seminary.

THE REVEREND BETTY WHITTED HOLLEY, Ph.D., Senior Presiding Elder, Ohio-South Ohio Conference, in the Columbus-Springfield-Xenia District, Third Episcopal District of the AMEC; superintending thirty churches. Dr. Holley is an Associate Professor at Payne Theological Seminary; Director for the Master of Divinity Degree Program at Payne.

THE REVEREND BRENDA BECKFORD PAYNE, Ph.D. is a native of Washington, D.C.; BSN, RN, M.Div.; all from Boston University, Boston, MA; Church founder; 39 years in ministry; pastored four churches over 22-year span; currently serving as Presiding Elder in the African Methodist Episcopal Church; business owner of two enterprises: HANDYBIB, and distributor of Organo- organic health products; married for 37 years with three adult college degreed children.

THE REVEREND DARLENE SINGER SMITH, Presiding Elder of the Missouri Conference, St. Louis Columbia District, 5th Episcopal District where Bishop Clement W. Fugh is the Presiding Prelate. She served as a Pastor for over 28 successful years, and four charges before being assigned a Presiding Elder. She is a published author, " The Spirit of Using What You Have."

THE REVEREND JACQUELINE D. SMITH is the Presiding Elder of the Southwest Conference Celebrated Central District Georgia Conference of the Sixth Episcopal District in the African Methodist Episcopal Church. A native of Grady County, Cairo, Georgia, Presiding Elder

Smith was educated at Washington Consolidated High School. Her post-secondary education in Sociology was obtained from Thomas University and Bainbridge University, respectively.

THE REVEREND CARLENE SOBERS has worshipped in the AME Church for many years. She has served as the YPD President, Sunday School Superintendent, Youth Pastor, and Intercessory Prayer and Visitation Coordinator. She has served as the Pastor of Emmanuel AME and Sealy Memorial AME Church and is currently the first female Presiding Elder of the Barbados District.

THE REVEREND LINDA FAYE THOMAS MARTIN is Presiding Elder of the South Memphis District, West Tennessee Conference, Thirteenth Episcopal District. She was elected as First Female Leader of the General Conference Delegation from the 13th Episcopal District and in the African Methodist Episcopal Church for the 48th, 49th, and 50thSessions of the General Conferences 2008, 2012, and 2016. She has served twice as President of the Thirteenth Episcopal District Presiding Elder's Council 2007-2008 and 2012-2013. Mother of two (2) adult children, Mr. Rickey Clyde Martin, Louisville, Kentucky and Rev. Lula Marie Martin Sanderson, Memphis, Tennessee, and grandmother of three. She is a leader, writer, mentor, and compelling preacher.

THE REVEREND DR. JANET STURDIVANT is a woman of many firsts: She is the first woman to ever preach the Annual Sermon in the Mother Conference of African Methodism since its organization in 1817, the first woman to pastor Asbury AME Church, Chester, PA (June 2003); the first time that any Annual Conference in the AME Church had two female Presiding Elders serving in it, at the same time, and the first woman to host the Delaware Annual Conference in the First Episcopal District of the AME Church (2005). Presiding Elder Sturdivant graduated from Medaille College in Buffalo, New York, with a

B.S. (May 1986). She graduated with an M.Div. from Lutheran Theological Seminary-Philadelphia (May 1993). She also received her D.Min. at Lutheran Theological Seminary-Philadelphia (May 2008).

THE REVEREND ROSETTA SWINTON, a native of Charleston, South Carolina, is currently pursuing an M.Div. at Grand Canyon University, *AZ*. Rosetta is a 10 1/2-year full-time missionary, serving in Malawi, Central Africa, 20th Episcopal District, Pastor of the McAllister A.M.E. International Worship Centre and Presiding Elder of the Mountain Moving Mulanje District, Malawi, Malawi South Annual Conference.

THE PRESIDING ELDER VALARIE J. WALKER was born in Winter Haven, Florida. She is a gifted preacher, teacher, administrator, workshop leader, evangelist, writer, and Presiding Elder. God's favor smiled on her on September 26, 2014, and she was appointed the first female Presiding Elder of the Orlando District of the Central Conference of the 11th Episcopal District of the AME Church.

THE PRESIDING ELDER LETITIA WATFORD Is both a practicing dentist and a Presiding Elder in the AME Church. A Phi Beta Kap pa graduate of Howard University (DDS), she was awarded her D.Min. degree from Samford University. She serves the Tuskegee District in the 9th Episcopal District. She is the spouse of Tom Watford, mother of Geneva and Justin Lawrence, and grand mother of Sophie.

BIBLIOGRAPHY

- Allen, R. Journal Article, "Our Own Vine, and Fig Tree: The Authority of History." Carolyn S. Beck. *Review of Religious Research*. Volume 29. No. 4. *Black American Religion in the Twentieth Century* (June 1988).

- Beck, Carolyn S. "Our Own Vine and Fig Tree: The Authority of History and Kinship in Mother Bethel." *Review of Religious Research*, Vol. 29, No. 4, 1988, pp. 369–384. *JSTOR*, www.jstor.org/stable/3511576.

- Blackaby, Henry T., Richard Blackaby, and Claude V. King, *Experiencing God: Knowing and Doing the Will of God*. Nashville, TN: B&H Publishing Group, 2008.

- Bonaparte, Yvette L. "A Perspective on Transformative Leadership and African American Women in History," *The Journal of Value-Based Leadership*, Vol 8, Issue 2 Summer/Fall 2015.

- Brown, Teresa Fry: *Can a Sistah Get a Little Help?: Encouragement for Black Women in Ministry,* The Pilgrim Press, 2008 Cleveland.

- Byfield, E. Anne Henning, "Preparing Leaders for Leadership," AHB Press 2005 Indianapolis, pg. 7.

- Carson, Clayborne and Peter Holloran, *A Knock at Midnight: Inspiration from Great Sermons of Reverend Martin Luther King, Jr.* New York, NY: Warner Books, 2001.

- Cooperation: *New Designs and Dynamics*. Palo Alto, CA: Stanford Business Books.

- Covey, S. https://wikidiff.com/transformational/transfomative, and Covey, Stephen, *Principle-centered Leadership*. New York: Simon and Schuster, 1992. Print.

- D. L. Cooperrider (Eds.), *Handbook of Transformative Leadership.* Encyclopedia.http://classic.studylight.org/enc/isb/icw.egi?numbcr=T6062.

- Lindsay. Gospelmusicchannel 8 "The Best of Shekinah Glory," February 19, 2012. www.youtube.com Accessed March 9, 2019.

- Go - RSV Search Results for "Go." Retrieved fromhttps://www.blueletter_bible.org// search/search.cfm?Criteria=Go&t=RSV#s=s_primary_O_1.

- Graham, P. (2003). *Mary Parker Follett: Prophet of management.*

- Frederick, l\.1D: Beard Group.

- King, Jr, M. L. "The Drum Major Instinct." Kamatube. February 4, 1968, copy.

- _____. Martin Luther King, Jr. quotes. Thinkex.ist.com. Accessed March 9, 2019. left @2016. KarmaTube.org. Accessed March 9, 2019.

- Ludema, J. D., & Cox, C. K. (2007). "Leadership for World Benefit: New Horizons for Research and Practice." In S. K. Piderit, R. E. Fry, & Orr, J. (1915). *Ministry*. International Standard Bible. TM. (2018) Ministry. https://www.biblestudytools.com /dictionary/ministry/

- McKenzie, Vashti M. *Not Without A Struggle.* The Pilgrim Press, 2012 Cleveland.

- Orr, James. Success.com. Accessed March 9, 2016. (1915). *Ministry.* International Standard Bible.

- Sweat, Lydia. October 13, 2016, "19 Powerful Quotes to Inspire Greatness and Success." The Division of Christian Education of the National Council of the Churches of Christ in the United States of America Transformational/transformative https://wikidiff com/transformational/ transformative.

- Transformative Leadership Achieving Unparalleled Excellence, https://www.researchgate.net /publication/257541719.

- WikiDiiff reference. wikidiff.com/transformational/transformative.

- Winfrey, Oprah. *Failure Is Another Steppingstone to Greatness: 110 Pages Personal Composition Journal Notebook with Motivational Quotes*. Independently Published, 2019.

ENDNOTES

1. Carolyn S. Beck, "Our Own Vine and Fig Tree: The Authority of History and Kinship in Mother Bethel." *Review of Religious Research*, vol. 29, no. 4, 1988, pp. 369–384. *JSTOR*, www.jstor.org/stable/3511576. Accessed 8 Apr. 2020.

2. Henry T. Blackaby, Richard Blackaby, and Claude V. King, *Experiencing God: Knowing and Doing the Will of God* (Nashville, TN: B&H Publishing Group, 2008), 3.

3. Yvette L. Bonaparte, "A Perspective on Transformative Leadership and African American Women in History, *The Journal of Value-Based Leadership*, vol 8, Issue 2 Summer/Fall 2015, xi.

4. Oprah Winfrey, *"Failure is Another Steppingstone to Greatness:" 110 Pages Personal Composition Journal Notebook with Motivational Quotes* (Independently Published, 2019).

5. Clayborne Carson and Peter Holloran, *A Knock at Midnight: Inspiration from Great Sermons of Reverend Martin Luther King, Jr.* (New York, NY: Warner Books, 2001), 174.

Reflections